Praise for

Hoop Tales:

UConn Huskies Men's Basketball

"I've been hooked on UConn basketball since I was a newly-arrived seventeen-year-old freshman at Litchfield Hall in the Jungle in 1961 and I spotted another newly-arrived freshman named Toby Kimball. He was 6'9" and bald and I decided my new school might be pretty good at this sport. The ride since then has been nothing but a wonder and Bob Porter and Wayne Norman describe it all in this terrific book. I not only have read it, but sleep with it under my pillow every night."

—Leigh Montville, former *Sports Illustrated* senior writer and coauthor of *Dare to Dream: Connecticut's Remarkable March to the National Championship*

Hoop Tales™ Series

Hoop Tales:

UConn Huskies Men's Basketball

Wayne Norman and Robert Porter

INSIDERS' GUIDE®

GUILFORD, CONNECTICUT
AN IMPRINT OF THE GLOBE PEQUOT PRESS

INSIDERS' GUIDE ®

Copyright © 2005 by The Globe Pequot Press

Hoop Tales is a trademark of Morris Book Publishing, LLC.

Text design: Casey Shain
Cover photos: University of Connecticut Division of Athletics,
except center right courtesy University of Connecticut Archives

Library of Congress Cataloging-in-Publication Data
Norman, N. Wayne.
    Hoop Tales : UConn Huskies men's basketball /
Wayne Norman and Robert Porter. — 1st ed.
        p. cm. — (Hoop tales series)
    ISBN 0-7627-3785-9
    1. Connecticut Huskies (basketball team) 2. University
of Connecticut—Basketball. I. Porter, Robert S. II. Title.
III. Series.

GV885.43.U44N67 2005
796.323'63'09746—dc22   2004060726

Manufactured in the United States of America
First Edition/First Printing

To Leighton B. Porter, 1914–1998
UConn Class of 1936, Freshman Basketball 1932–33
For sixty-six years, as loyal a fan as UConn ever had

To Marcie B. Mason
For fifty-six years, as loyal a mom as anyone ever had

Contents

Preface

On March 31, 1988, in Botswana's beautiful Chobe Game Park, my friend Wayne Norman and I stood under starlit skies and scanned the dial of a shortwave radio. We were trying to learn sports scores from the USA via Armed Forces Radio, specifically the result of the 1988 NIT Championship game played the night before in Madison Square Garden between Ohio State and our beloved Connecticut Huskies. Wayne's trip to Botswana had been arranged months earlier, based on the expected end of Husky basketball and therefore his radio broadcasts.

The shortwave scan from the African game park was futile, so we had to wait four days before calling my parents in New Milford, Connecticut, some 10,000 miles away. In 1988 there was no Internet and certainly no international version of ESPN to provide scores. My mother's voice cracked with emotion as she spoke of UConn player Jeff King sitting on the rim of a basket in Madison Square Garden; she was apparently unaware that we still did not know who had won. Finally, my father, a UConn graduate who played freshman basketball there in 1932–33, said: *"Yes, yes—They won the NIT!!!!!!!"*

It was elation for my parents and me but somewhat bittersweet for Wayne, since he missed the broadcasts he would have relished. Like virtually all others connected with the Huskies, he assumed by late March UConn's season would be over, given a 14 and 13 regular-season record. It had been six years since the Huskies had played basketball after the Big East Tournament. Instead, to quote former UConn coach Dee Rowe, who filled in for Wayne on the radio broadcasts, the Huskies went on a "magic carpet ride" under then second-year head coach Jim Calhoun.

The 1988 African experience sealed our UConn basketball bond and tightened our already close friendship. Wayne has now broadcast more UConn Network games than anyone and was honored for his 1,000th game in September of 2004. I continued with my international banking career, following the Huskies not only in Botswana, but later in Indonesia, Uganda, Russia, Armenia, Ukraine, Philippines, Australia, and Pakistan, while always trying to adjust my overseas travel to be home for the NCAA Tournament.

Looking back, that 1988 NIT Championship was the first of many magic carpet rides that would follow. The years from 1988 through 2004 have given Connecticut basketball fans arguably more thrills than fans of any other college team. The UConn fight song has been heard countless times on national telecasts celebrating memorable Husky hoops triumphs.

However, UConn basketball did not begin with that NIT Championship. Jim Calhoun took Connecticut from a regional to a national program, but the coach himself speaks enthusiastically about the deep New England college basketball roots that he vividly remembers, including games he played against the Huskies in the 1960s.

In considering this book, Wayne and I believed there was a lot to be told about those earlier seasons that had such a major part in UConn becoming the top-tier national program it is today. We chose to go back fifty years to a huge upset when the Huskies defeated then national power Holy Cross on their seemingly invincible home court in Worcester. Interviewing and researching for that 1954 game was followed by extensive talks with others who brought memorable moments to Husky fans in later years.

Together Wayne and I have some eighty-six years of UConn basketball knowledge. My own memory goes back to listening on radio at age nine to the late George Ehrlich on WTIC describing a UConn first-round NCAA loss to Syracuse in 1957. My personal passion was such that in Russia in the mid-1990s, I joked with American colleagues that my only fear in life was they would carve on my tombstone: HE NEVER LIVED TO SEE UCONN PLAY IN THE FINAL FOUR. Of course Coach Calhoun and many others quickly made that quip vanish.

For those who cheered, rejoiced, or even shed the occasional tear for the Huskies, I hope the stories that follow bring you enjoyment.

—Robert Porter

As Toby Kimball was rewriting the UConn record books in 1965, I was living in Glendale, California, and frankly had never heard of Kimball or the University of Connecticut. In fact, when my father was transferred to

Bridgeport, Connecticut, in the summer of 1965, one of my first friends in Connecticut told me he was going to UConn. Thinking he meant someplace near Alaska, I replied, "Why don't you go somewhere around here?"

Eventually, I followed him to Storrs, and while I didn't see Kimball play, I saw plenty of great players at the Field House during my days as a student. But my first close relationship with Husky hoops came during the 1969–70 season. Working with Robert Porter on WHUS radio broadcasts, we got to know first-year coach Dee Rowe—and to this day we remain close to Dee. The final game of that season remains one of the most special memories I have of UConn basketball. In fact Coach Rowe has a photo taken after that game of Bob Staak cutting down the nets, and I can be seen holding him up. We tell the story of that game and that season in this book.

I remained close to Connecticut basketball through the 1970s. And in 1979 the president of the Connecticut Radio Network, Barry Berman, offered me the opportunity to broadcast UConn games on his statewide network. I never dreamed I'd still be doing games some twenty-five years later. Thanks, Barry!

Being as close as I am to UConn basketball, cowriting this book was a privilege. It helped refresh my memory on games I had seen but had gotten hazy on—particularly the 1990 Dream Season. But more important, I loved learning about the names, the games, and the stories of some terrific UConn teams from the years when I was living in California.

Yes, there are two NCAA Men's Championship banners hanging at Gampel Pavilion. Broadcasting those title games were two of the best nights of my life (with the

2004 Boston Red Sox World Series win not far behind!). But this book is about more than those championships. It shows what Jim Calhoun has built in Storrs, but it also makes it clear that there were successful teams and a passion for UConn basketball long before Calhoun's arrival in May of 1986.

The book was a labor of love for Robert and me, and we only hope that you learn as much from it as we did.

—Wayne Norman

Acknowledgments

For two first-time authors, a large amount of assistance and support was given and is greatly appreciated. The entire UConn basketball community, starting with head coach Jim Calhoun, gave full cooperation. Special thanks go to associate directors of athletics Tim Tolokan and Mike Enright, each of whom provided valuable assistance, as did Mark Roy of University Communications.

Arnold Dean and Joe D'Ambrosio of WTIC radio were generous with their time and memories. Thanks also go to WTIC for allowing the use of quotes from exclusive interviews done while on their payroll. We wish to acknowledge Connecticut Public Television for allowing us to quote from their superb video on the history of UConn basketball and John Tuite for allowing quotes from the "Field House Memories" audio tape produced for WILI radio.

Mike Urban, Mary Norris, and Josh Rosenberg of the Globe Pequot Press were very helpful in guiding us through this process and being supportive in all ways, especially to expedite publication.

Long-time UConn basketball fan and supporter Eli Dunn provided invaluable editorial assistance.

Every living UConn head basketball coach was generous with his time for interviews. Several key assistant coaches from 1954 through the present provided numerous insights into the fifty years covered in this book. Special thanks go to founder of the Big East Conference Dave Gavitt and long-time Connecticut director of athletics John Toner for their input on key stages in the development of UConn basketball.

The numerous players interviewed for this book ranged in era from the articulate Worthy Patterson, captain of the 1953–54 team, to the enthusiastic Rashad Anderson, a sophomore on the 2004 championship team.

A final and very special thanks goes to former head coach and presently special adviser for athletics Dee Rowe. No one in the UConn athletic community is more beloved than Coach Rowe. Without Dee's extensive support and encouragement, this book could not have been written.

The 1954 Holy Cross Upset

The question is posed to an all-time great UConn player of the mid-1950s, Art Quimby: "Would the 1954 win over Holy Cross in Worcester be the equivalent to fifty years later UConn going to Cameron Indoor Stadium and beating Duke on the road?" His answer: "A definitive yes."

Of course, Connecticut basketball was not invented on the night of February 27, 1954. Yet, looking back at Husky hoops history from the post–World War II era, this was the game that established UConn as a successful and serious regional power.

What made this road victory so special was the quality of the opponent. During the 1940s and 1950s, Holy Cross was the reigning king of New England college basketball and a national power. Their 1947 team, coached by Doggie Julian, won the NCAA Championship and finished 27–3. A freshman on that team was Bob Cousy. The Crusaders were New England's only national champion until UConn's first title fifty-two years later in 1999.

The 1946–47 season was also the first year of a new professional league called the National Basketball Association. One of its members was the Boston Celtics. Holy Cross basketball was so highly regarded that some fans doubted Boston's new pro team could beat the Crusaders. During its early era, the NBA had a system of draft picks based on region to build up fan interest. Between 1947 and 1962, five All-Americans from Holy Cross would go on to play for the Celtics. In chronological order they were: George Kaftan from the 1947 NCAA Champions, the immortal Cousy, Togo Palazzi in 1954, Tommy Heinsohn in 1956 who became NBA rookie of the year, and Jack "The Shot" Foley in 1962.

With senior Palazzi and sophomore Heinsohn as the stars, plus plenty of depth, the 1953–54 Crusader team was as good as any during its long reign as the best of New England. The final record of 26–2 is still the best in school history. The prior year they had reached the NCAA East Regional Finals, but in those days the NCAA Tournament was often upstaged by the Madison Square Garden–based NIT. The Crusaders, like UConn, made appearances in both tournaments during the 1950s.

If talent alone was not enough to intimidate opponents, Holy Cross had an enormous home court advantage in the Worcester Auditorium. It was actually more a theatrical setting than a basketball venue with its concert hall configuration, and it barely seated 3,000 people. As Connecticut would repeatedly learn in the 1950s and 1960s, winning at "The Aud" would be the toughest task on the regular-season schedule.

While Holy Cross was the premier New England team, by the mid-1950s UConn had already proven itself to be a regional power, thanks to the man universally credited as the father of Connecticut basketball, Hugh Greer.

On December 20, 1946, six games into the season, Connecticut head basketball coach Blair Gullion shocked the university by resigning effective immediately to take the same post with Washington University in St. Louis. UConn athletics director George Van Bibber promoted freshman coach Greer, a graduate of the class of 1926, to head varsity coach. Greer's team responded by winning the remaining twelve games on the schedule.

Hugh Greer is remembered fondly by all who knew him. Husky standout Worthy Patterson said of Greer, "He had an interest in us off the court. In the summer he gave some players use of his house, so we could attend summer school for the credits we needed." Art Quimby said Greer's word was his bond.

Burr Carlson, who played for Greer in 1951–52 and was a UConn head coach in the late 1960s, recalled the era. "There were so little resources that his wife, Billie, who was a fantastic lady, helped scout players for him."

Nick Rodis, an assistant to Greer from 1954 to 1962, described the head coach: "He was a gentleman, a very hard worker, intelligent, very popular, and so very helpful to others. I could not get over his premature and sudden passing months after I left UConn." Rodis also has memories of UConn's difficulties with Holy Cross and Greer's dry wit. "One time we are playing them and go down by 12–0 or something like that. He turns to me and says, 'I think we are going to get shut out,' but no matter what, Hugh Greer was completely composed at all times on the bench."

As a member of the newly formed Yankee Conference starting in 1947, Greer's next six Husky teams compiled an overall record of 112–35. In those years they won four Yankee Conference Championships, and this era included Connecticut's first NCAA appearance on March 20, 1951—a 63–52 loss to St. John's at New York's Madison Square Garden.

On February 12, 1952, the Hugh Greer–led Huskies traveled to Worcester to face Holy Cross for the first time since the 1930–31 season. As expected, UConn lost 72–53. But a year later, Connecticut won its first eight games, and the visit by Holy Cross to Storrs was highly anticipated. In those pre–Field House days, UConn played home games in an ROTC facility known as the "Hangar." Patterson loved playing at the old Hangar. "It was really a Quonset hut with a very low ceiling and lots of crowd noise." The January 7, 1953, home game with Holy Cross led to an overflow crowd, and a mini-riot resulted as students tried to get in. The game was competitive, but Holy Cross again emerged victorious by a score of 71–67.

Greer and his players knew the following season might be special. The Huskies had a first-rate scoring combination in junior center Art Quimby and quick senior forward Patterson. "We were a cocky bunch," Patterson recalled for a Connecticut Public Television special on UConn basketball more than forty years later. "We had Jimmy Ahern who had transferred from a Seton Hall team that had won something like thirty games, and we also had Ronnie Bushwell, another very good transfer from St. John's."

Connecticut won its first fourteen games and started to get attention. This resulted in the then infant "game of the

Worthy Patterson, captain of the 1953–54 Huskies. *(University of Connecticut Division of Athletics)*

The Holy Cross Crusaders—UConn's Nemesis

The two teams have not played since 1988, and UConn won ten of the last sixteen meetings. But from 1952 through 1973, Holy Cross dominated the Huskies like no other team has before or especially since. Between 1956 and 1968, the teams played a home-and-home series, so in the more than two-decade span, they met thirty-six times. The Crusaders won twenty-nine of those games, including a seven-game streak from 1960 to 1963 and a twelve-game streak from 1966 to 1973. Of the fifteen teams UConn has met fifty or more times, only five hold a lifetime edge over UConn, through 2004, as follows:

Holy Cross 42 wins, UConn 21 wins

Syracuse 44 wins, UConn 28 wins

St. John's 32 wins, UConn 21 wins

Georgetown 29 wins, UConn 23 wins

Villanova 29 wins, UConn 24 wins

week" telecast being switched away from an Ivy League contest to UConn visiting Fordham at its Rose Hill Gym in New York on February 3, 1954. "We were two of the four undefeated teams in the country," said Patterson, "so the game attracted quite a bit of interest." Fordham handed the Huskies their first loss of the year, 70–63. "Then we have to get on a bus and go to Colgate, and I remember lots of snow and a tough, long trip," added Patterson. "Colgate had a substitute guard also named Patterson, and he came off the bench and his shooting killed us." The 74–68 loss would be the second and last of the regular season.

UConn won its next six games, only adding to the buildup for the late-season visit to Holy Cross. By the time the Huskies took the bus to Worcester on the last Saturday in February, they were a sparkling 20–2. However, The Cross, as they were commonly known, had an even better record at 22–1. Add to this a forty-seven–game winning streak at Worcester Auditorium, and Holy Cross was a heavy favorite.

Quimby recalled, "We did not fear them, but to say we were confident, I'd say no. Their coach Buster Sherry was one of the best, and with Palazzi, Heinsohn, and Ronnie Perry Sr., they were always ranked in the top ten nationally."

Quimby himself was recruited by Holy Cross, but the Crusaders wanted him to wait a year before joining them. "They had a policy of recruiting a group only every two years and holding them together. I did not want to sit out a year, so I chose UConn. We had a great backcourt that year with Jimmy Ahern as a great passer, and Worthy had an incredibly quick first step to the basket."

The game more than lived up to its billing. The Huskies started well, taking an early lead, but Holy Cross then took control and moved out to a 26–17 advantage. Connecticut rallied late in the first half to take a 41–40 half-time lead.

The second half was tight throughout. As the minutes wound down, Quimby scored seven straight points. It was a one-point game going into the final minute when Quimby scored again to put UConn up 76–75 with 57 seconds left. The Crusaders missed on their next possession with UConn rebounding, but Ron Perry Sr. stole the ball from Patterson and scored with 14 seconds remaining to regain the lead at 77 to 76.

Patterson remembered an oddity in the game's final minute. "The ball rolled under the stands, and it could not be retrieved, so they had to get another one out of a bag, and both teams had to agree which ball was suitable. It took longer than a normal time-out to settle on which one would be used."

Greer called time-out, and he set up a play for Patterson. Quimby recalled it for CPTV, "The play was to get the ball to Worthy and for the rest of us to get out of the way."

Patterson did pretty well with the new basketball. Years later he recounted for CPTV, "Someone came right at me once I got the ball, and I just went around him and laid it up. And when it went through the net, it was like, YES — and the place went wild."

The clock ran out before Holy Cross could inbound the ball, and the small visiting contingent from Storrs cele-brated UConn's 78–77 win, ending the Crusaders' long home winning streak. The victory ensured that New England now had two legitimate basketball powers.

Coach Greer and Captain Patterson from the 1953–54 team.
(University of Connecticut Archives)

However, the two teams went separate ways after the regular season. The first postseason college basketball tournament was the NIT formed in 1938 by New York's Metropolitan Basketball Writers Association. The NCAA Tournament did not begin play until the following year. In the 1950s the NIT was an appealing choice, especially to eastern teams, and there was also the allure of all games being played in the college hoops mecca of the old Madison Square Garden. Thus, three fine Holy Cross teams, in 1952, 1954, and 1955, chose the NIT. The 1954 team that fell to UConn at home

Who Was the National Champ in 1954???

Many of today's college sports fans vigorously complain about the often controversial Bowl Championship Series (BCS) that determines the college football champion. But the BCS of today looks good in comparison to college basketball in 1954, when no fewer than three teams had a legitimate claim to the title. The fuss started when unbeaten and number one–ranked Kentucky refused to go to the NCAA Tournament after three of its key seniors were declared ineligible. The NCAA had determined they were postgraduates. Without the Wildcats, LaSalle won the NCAA Tournament. However, the Holy Cross team that UConn had upset in late February also had a strong case after winning the NIT, where three of the top eight ranked teams played. The final AP poll that year showed the following rankings (records include postseason play):

1. Kentucky with a 25–0 record and no postseason play

2. La Salle with a 26–4 record and NCAA Championship

3. Holy Cross with a 26–2 record and NIT Championship

went on to win that year's NIT with a 71–62 victory over Duquesne in the championship game.

"We wanted to go to the NIT also," said Patterson. "Most of our players were from Greater New York, and I was from Greenwich. We were not crazy about having to travel up to Buffalo for the NCAA."

The visit to Buffalo was UConn's second appearance in the NCAAs. The opponent was Navy. Patterson added, "They were supposed to have this limit on height at Navy, but it sure didn't seem like it, given the size of their players." The Huskies led at the half 40–38, with Patterson and Quimby leading UConn in scoring with 21 and 19 points respectively, but it still was not enough as Navy won 85–80. It was the last game for senior Worthy Patterson.

After leaving UConn, Patterson was the last player cut by the Celtics in his first attempt at the NBA. However, he later made the St. Louis Hawks and played with such NBA stars as Bob Pettit and Cliff Hagan. "I remember my grand-father looking in amazement at my first NBA paycheck. He could not believe you could actually get paid for playing basketball."

The calendar year 1954 still had one more treat in store for the UConn faithful. On December 1, the brand new center-of-campus Field House opened with a 116–77 rout of Rhode Island. Observers from the time felt it was the finest campus basketball facility in New England; it *was* one of the largest, with seating for nearly 5,000.

With UConn again having a stellar season, there was another huge buildup for the late-season visit by Holy Cross in the next to last game on February 26, 1955. It was again a close game, with the Crusaders exacting revenge by a 60–58 score over the Huskies in the new Field House. Both teams accepted NIT bids that year. Holy Cross was one of four seeded teams in the twelve-team field but was upset by St. Francis in its opening game.

UConn made its NIT debut on March 12, 1955, with a high-scoring loss to St. Louis, 110–103. Art Quimby scored 18 points with 21 rebounds in his final UConn game. Quimby led the nation in rebounding in both his junior and senior years. Some long-time UConn observers still feel Quimby was as good as any UConn basketball player before Jim Calhoun arrived as coach. UConn's star player of the early to mid-1960s Toby Kimball said he looked up to Quimby as he was growing up.

Quimby is still active and lives in eastern Connecticut. He spent many years as an educator working with the state's vocational education system. He also reached the rank of full colonel in the Reserves, which started with his UConn ROTC participation.

After Quimby's playing days, Greer coached winning seasons at UConn in seven of his last eight years. His life was tragically cut short by a heart attack in January 1963 after playing handball with assistant coach George Wigton. Greer coached from the end of 1946 until his death just over sixteen years later. His record as head coach was 286 wins with only 112 losses and thirteen Yankee Conference Championships (counting the year of his midseason death). Until Jim Calhoun, no Connecticut coach came close to his totals. UConn named the now multipurpose Field House after Hugh Greer.

*Art Quimby (25), the first great UConn star, battles a University of
New Hampshire Wildcat for the ball. (University of Connecticut Archives)*

But if Greer were still alive, it seems certain his fondest
memory would be that Saturday night in Worcester in 1954.
More than fifty years later that game still brings back smiles
to Quimby and Patterson. Even with all the glory for
UConn basketball in the half century since, it's hard to
come up with a more meaningful or exciting regular-season
win. From that night on, UConn was on the map of quality
basketball.

" . . . Stolen by Perno"

"Over to Bradley . . . double-teamed, holds the ball
. . . Stolen by Perno . . . Dom Perno steals from
Bradley with 18 seconds to go. Perno dribbles to the
right, holds the ball . . . over to Dellasala in the
corner . . . 14 seconds to go . . . in the corner to
Perno, now to Slomcenski . . . 10 seconds to go . . .
in the corner now . . . 7 seconds, 6 seconds. Now to
Kimball . . . feeds to Perno with 3 seconds—who
shoots—no good . . . the rebound . . . there's the gun
. . . UConn has won 52–50. The Huskies go into the
Finals of the East. Wow!!!!"

—WTIC's George Ehrlich describing
the last 20 seconds of UConn's 1964 upset win over
Princeton in the NCAA Tournament

During the NCAA tournament of 2000, WFAN's Chris "Mad Dog" Russo interviewed Bill Bradley, then running for president, regarding his NCAA Tournament memories with Princeton. By any measure Bradley was one of the ten greatest college basketball players in history, probably in the top five. Russo and Bradley discussed how the future U.S. senator led Princeton to the Final Four in his senior year. Then the Mad Dog asked, "Now, looking here at the record book, it shows in your junior year [1964] you lost to Connecticut. Can you tell me anything about that game?"

"All I remember is that it was a bad game. I cannot remember any details, except it was a bad game," Bradley replied.

It might have been a bad and forgettable game for Bradley, but for UConn, it was simply the single most memorable win in all the years prior to the 1986 arrival of Jim Calhoun. Five days earlier, in the NCAA opening round, UConn had upset Temple 53–48 in the Owls' home city of Philadelphia, sending the Huskies against the heavily favored Ivy League Champion.

For then senior cocaptain and future UConn head coach Dom Perno from New Haven, his most famous moment as a player is much clearer than Bradley's memory of the game's end. "My foul shots were really what I remember best. I was a pretty good all-around player with my floor game, passing, and defense, but I could not shoot much at all. Princeton had come back to tie us at 50–50, and I was fouled with just over 30 seconds to go. My knees were weak for the first one, and the damn thing hits the front rim, bounces off the backboard and then somehow drops through. The second was nothing but net, and we go up by two."

Perno then recalls what happened next. "We are in a 1-2-2 zone with Dan 'Spider' Hesford at the point, and I am on the left wing. Bradley gets the ball of course, but Spider had been a huge pest to him the whole game, so he does not notice me on the double-team. He holds the ball over his head, and I'm able to swipe it away when he's not looking. But then I shoot at the very end, and every time I shot Shabel has a near seizure."

Fred Shabel, then in his first year as UConn coach, agrees. "Dom was great at everything but shooting. My memory is that with some ten minutes to go in the Princeton game, I said to Dom, 'One more shot and you are out.'" But as the record shows, Perno played well enough to be one of three Huskies to play the full forty minutes against Princeton, though he shot just 4 for 15 for the game.

"I just remember how thankful I was the clock had run out," said Shabel. "We had had the lead and control most of the game, but they were finishing strong. Had the game lasted much longer, I did not like our chances. The defenses we played were always a hybrid of man-to-man and zones, and for Princeton we played some box-and-1, in order to try and somewhat contain Bradley." The strategy worked for most of the game as Bradley shot only 6 for 15 from the floor. The *Hartford Courant* story the next day said it was believed to be his season low. However, Shabel recalls Princeton changed tactics by having Bradley bring up the ball. "Our box-and-1 would no longer work then, and it seemed good things happened for Princeton each time he brought the ball up court." Bradley finished with 22 total

The Origins of the Pep Band

Former UConn coach Fred Shabel credits his own mentor, Duke head coach Vic Bubas, with innovation in all aspects of college basketball. Shabel recalled that Bubas had been extremely impressed with UCLA's pep band and synchronized dancing cheerleaders for building fan excitement. Bubas thus took the UCLA model and brought it to Duke, and Shabel did the same thing when he came to UConn. Thus on December 4, 1963, the UConn pep band made its debut at the Field House for the home opener against American International College. "We had the straw hats and the whole works," said Shabel, "and I feel it added a lot to the spirit of the Field House in those days. We were probably the first school in the northeast with a pep band."

Forty years later it is impossible to imagine any UConn home game or major tournament game without the pep band playing the UConn fight song and its steady repertoire of familiar upbeat tunes to the Husky faithful. After all, what would still another Big East title or even National Championship be without the pep band playing the spine-tingling UConn fight song as Husky players and fans celebrate together?

Dom Perno shoots from the corner against Princeton as Bill Bradley (42) watches. (University of Connecticut Division of Athletics)

points, 10 under his season average. He connected on 10 of 11 from the foul line, while also playing the full forty minutes.

While Perno had his full moment of glory, the star and team MVP in the mid-1960s era was power forward Toby Kimball from Sudbury, Massachusetts. He also played the entire game against Princeton and had team highs with 16 points and 13 rebounds.

Kimball recalled the three Huskies playing the full forty minutes (the third being senior center Ed Slomcenski of Naugatuck). "We were young and energetic, and we took pretty good care of ourselves. Coach Shabel worked us very hard in practice, so when game-time came, it was fun to play."

With regard to Bradley, the UConn star said, "I think he had a bit of an off night. Spider Hesford really did put on his tentacles when he covered somebody. He would tie you up in knots. Our strategy was to let their other guys beat us."

Shabel also remembers UConn being disrespected by Princeton coach Bill van Breda Kolff, who later coached the Lakers. "He didn't even watch our win over Temple," said Shabel, "and when asked about us, he replied, 'How good can a team be when it only scores in the 50s?'—so it was all the sweeter when we won 52–50."

What might seem shocking forty years later is that this game was *not* televised in Connecticut. Thus the voice of long-time WTIC UConn play-by-play announcer George Ehrlich remains vivid to the many in the state who still recall the upset.

Perhaps it took die-hard UConn fans a few minutes to digest the magnitude of this win. Here was a team that lost ten regular-season games and had to go on the road to win a Yankee Conference playoff game just to get into the national tournament. Then, in the span of five days under a thirty-one-year-old first-year head coach, UConn won two NCAA Tournament games. Prior to this, UConn had won only one NCAA game—under legendary coach Hugh Greer, who was 1 and 8 in NCAA play. How did this happen?

Fred Shabel arrived at UConn in 1963, after playing at Duke and then being a top assistant for six seasons. "I fully respected all Hugh Greer had done to build the UConn program over many years," he says, "but it still needed an upgrade. We needed to introduce promoting the program and a greater sense of excitement. We ran lots of basketball clinics all over the area and other activities to raise the visibility of UConn basketball."

"Nobody knew me," laughed Shabel upon reflection. "Early in the season, we are hosting Boston College at home, with their new head coach Bob Cousy, who had just finished his stellar Celtics career. I walk out to take my seat on the bench with silence from the crowd, and then Cousy enters and gets a standing ovation from our own fans in the Field House." Shabel did not mention his Huskies went on to clobber Boston College, 108–81.

Shabel had inherited a seasoned team that had reached the NCAA Tournament the prior year under George Wigton, an interim coach. Wigton had taken over in January of 1963 after Hugh Greer's untimely death. Shabel knew instantly he had one genuine star in Toby Kimball.

"I already had my classes picked out at North Carolina," recalled Kimball from his present home in a San Diego suburb, and UConn was not even in the picture after a point-shaving scandal in 1961. "But my Dad said 'Don't rush to conclusions,' and when I met Hugh Greer, I saw a man devastated by the scandal but also determined to move forward. Greer made it clear to my Dad and me that UConn had been strong in the past and this isn't going to stop us," added Kimball. "I was sold."

"Another small thing made a difference to me," said Kimball. "At North Carolina they only showed me the campus for twenty minutes and then it was straight to the gym. At UConn I was shown classes and met professors, so I was much more impressed with their overall approach."

Shabel quickly determined his 1963–64 players did not have great overall team speed, but they had good defense and excellent rebounding, the latter due mainly to Kimball but also to 6'11" senior cocaptain Ed Slomcenski. Every former player interviewed used the word "genius" to describe Shabel. He adjusted his tactics to exactly fit his personnel, thus the two low-scoring NCAA wins. The next season, when senior Kimball was joined by some good shooting sophomores, the per game scoring average soared to 85.1 points per game—fourth highest in UConn history.

Despite the veteran talent and the skilled new coach, the regular season was bumpy, to say the least. UConn lost several very close games, including two to Holy Cross, and one each to Yale, Boston University, Massachusetts, and Rutgers. Against archrival Rhode Island, the Huskies split the two regular-season games and tied the Rams for the Yankee Conference title. UConn had to play at Rhode Island for a playoff to determine who would go to the NCAA and won by a point, 61–60. It was the first of two such Yankee Conference playoff games against Rhody within Shabel's first three seasons.

Shabel was not happy with UConn being sent to Philadelphia for the NCAA opener against Temple, virtually a home game for the Owls. In addition, Temple had beaten UConn by eight points in their regular-season matchup.

The 1963–64 team. (University of Connecticut Archives)

"Temple had a great rebounder in a guy named Jim Williams," recalled Kimball. "He was one of the four or five best players I ever played against." Shabel used his mixed defenses and slower pace throughout. UConn trailed at the half, 26–24. Both teams shot poorly. Kimball's 17 rebounds nearly offset 20 off the boards by Williams. But when the gun sounded (there were no buzzers in those days), UConn had won by five and was thus headed to the regionals in Raleigh, North Carolina.

Dom Perno recalled the plane trip. "We were actually on the same plane as the Princeton team. Their players were in the back, and I remember seeing Bradley who was already a nationally known superstar. He was immersed in a book the whole flight."

The upset win left the UConn players both exhausted and overjoyed. Through a hookup provided by UConn student radio station WHUS, players were immediately able to share the thrill with good buddies back at Storrs, the only place in the state where the game was actually seen via closed-circuit.

The good news was that UConn was now just one win away from the then unnamed Final Four. The bad news was that the opponent was their coach's former employer Duke, and the game was to be played the very next night just a few miles from the Duke campus.

"My only fond memory of that game was the warm-ups," recalled Perno. "Their drills were identical to ours, which showed us how much Coach Shabel had brought to UConn from Duke."

"They came at us in waves," said Kimball, "but part of it was that we had played our hearts out the night before against Princeton and had little gas left."

"My tactic of holding the ball to shorten the game totally failed against Duke's backcourt pressure," recalled Shabel. "If I had to do it over, I would have tried to quicken the pace, but they really were much better."

The box score shows a totally lopsided game from the very start, with Duke up an overwhelming 63–27 at the half and winning 101–54. Duke All-American Jeff Mullins poured in 30 points, and at his side was another future All-

"The Voice of the Huskies"— WTIC's George Ehrlich

When Connecticut's largest radio station, WTIC in Hartford, acquired the rights to broadcast UConn games in 1956, George Ehrlich of radio station WHAY in New Britain was brought over to do the play-by-play, and he did so up to 1974. In the mid-1950s, most Americans had television, but from the Rose Bowl on New Year's Day until Yankee or Red Sox baseball in April, there were virtually no televised sports in Connecticut. Thus the smooth and precise radio voice of George Ehrlich soon became identified with the growth in interest for UConn sports, especially the successful basketball teams of the late 1950s and through the 1960s. For most of his years doing UConn games, he was ably assisted by Floyd Richards, who was better known in the Greater Hartford area as entertainer Hap Richards. But it was Ehrlich who brought the magical moments of UConn basketball to thousands in his long play-by-play career.

Arnold Dean, long-time WTIC sportscaster, said, "George was so important to UConn in those early days, and I regret that he is now all but forgotten." Unfortunately, very little recorded tape remains from his broadcasts, but those thrilling final 20 seconds of the upset win over Princeton do exist, and they bring back to life the voice of a true professional.

American in Jack Marin, as well as two talented 6'11" big men in Jay Buckley and Hack Tison. Only Kimball with 18 points and 14 rebounds was in double digits in either category for UConn. That Duke team might have been their very best prior to the back-to-back national champions of the early 1990s. They soundly beat a highly regarded Michigan team with Cazzie Russell in the Final Four before finally bowing in the championship game to the first of the ten UCLA championships under John Wooden.

Even with the one-sided loss, UConn players were happily stunned to find more than a thousand fans cheering them upon arrival at Bradley Airport. "It was very moving," recalled Kimball in his San Diego–area home. "There was a fan base in the state of Connecticut that I still see there today."

In addition, the 1963–64 season began the many close links between Duke and UConn, now perhaps the top two national powers in the sport. As Perno and Kimball well recall, Shabel took the high standards of Duke basketball and brought them to UConn with immediate results. But an arcane statistic also stands out.

Starting with the defeat by the Blue Devils in the 1964 East Regional Finals, Duke and UConn have met five times in NCAA play with all of them being either Sweet Sixteen games or later—four of them being regional finals or in the Final Four. The 1964 game may have been lopsided, but three of the games that followed in 1990, 1999, and 2004 are among the all-time NCAA Tournament classics, and the two most recent duels bring instant smiles to tens of thousands of Husky fans.

Bill Bradley and Dom Perno together again in 1981. (University of Connecticut Archives/Dom Perno)

Yet it was the thrilling upset over Princeton that stands out in mid-1960s Husky hoop history. The recorded words of George Ehrlich in the final seconds, "*. . . stolen by Perno,*" might not be at quite the level in New England sports lore with "*. . . and Havlicek steals the ball,*" which took place only thirteen months later. But for the many Husky faithful of that time, it was indeed a night to long remember.

The Wes Bialosuknia Era

"He stops . . . he pops . . . SWISH . . . Bialosuknia scores from downtown Storrs . . ."

—WTIC's George Ehrlich numerous times
in the mid-1960s describing a 30-foot jumper by Wes
Bialosuknia in the old UConn Field House

He was more a loner than a leader; his defense was sometimes less than stellar; he didn't enjoy the physical side of the game; his pro career was briefer than anticipated, but he could shoot—oh my, could he ever shoot.

In basketball skills overall, Wes Bialosuknia was not an equal to the Ray Allen– or Rip Hamilton–level players of recent Connecticut vintage, but for the sheer ability to *electrify* a crowd, nobody, before or since at UConn, has come close.

"I coached major college basketball for ten years, six as an assistant at Duke, and four as UConn head coach," said Fred Shabel, "and only one player ever had a full-time unrestricted green light to shoot, and that was Wes. He was as good as any collegiate shooter I have ever seen." Shabel's words of praise do not come lightly, since at Duke he coached three All-Americans in Art Heyman, Jeff Mullins, and Jack Marin, all of whom had NBA careers.

The numbers speak for themselves; Wes was by far the all-time leading UConn scorer in points per game, with an average of 28.0 his senior year alone. Shabel added, "If there had been shot charts of his baskets, you'd have seen roughly 50 percent or more of his field goals would have been three-pointers had it existed." Thus it is reasonable to say that his senior year average would have been 33 or more under modern rules.

But like Joe DiMaggio, Sandy Koufax, and a few others, the statistics do not tell the whole story—you simply had to *see* Wes on a hot shooting night and *hear* the crowd when he lit up the Field House, especially the night of his final home game.

Fred Shabel and His Class of 1967

When Shabel left as the top assistant at Duke after a Final Four appearance by the Blue Devils in 1963, he wasted no time in putting together the best recruiting class UConn had ever seen. Bill Holowaty was a high school star from tiny Mohawk, New York, near Utica. He was eagerly recruited by North Carolina and nearby Syracuse. "I thought UConn was the place near Alaska the first time

Wes Bialosuknia, one of the greatest collegiate shooters ever.
(University of Connecticut Division of Athletics)

Fred Shabel phoned me, but the man could talk you into anything, and the next thing you know I am saying 'no' to Dean Smith and going to UConn."

Tommy Penders was the leading high school scorer in Connecticut his senior year at Stratford. He too was charmed by Shabel into going to UConn. "I thought of myself as a scorer, but I became a point guard with instructions to keep my eyes open for Wes when I had the ball. Wes only had eyes for the rim," laughed Penders.

Bialosuknia recalled Penders as being a huge overachiever and a solid player, who would always get him the ball whenever the Husky sharpshooter was open on fast breaks.

Shabel added Ron Ritter, the younger brother of Al Ritter, who had just completed three seasons of Husky basketball. Ron was another hotly contested recruit, sought by famous coach Lefty Drisell, then at Davidson. The incoming class also included Dick Thompson, a 6'7" center who could shoot like a guard, and an experienced twenty-five-year-old ball handler in ex-Marine P. J. Curran.

But the prize recruit was the 6'2" guard from Poughkeepsie, right across the New York state line. "Every college wanted to have Wes," Shabel recalled. "I really never thought we'd get him." But the story as remembered by Bialosuknia illustrates the exceptional determination and recruiting ability of Shabel.

Just as they had wanted Holowaty, Syracuse eagerly sought Bialosuknia. "In the spring of 1963, I went to Syracuse and was pressured by their Fred Lewis to accept a basketball scholarship, even though he knew I wanted to go to UConn," said Wes. "I came back to Poughkeepsie on a Sunday and on Monday Coach Shabel called and said he did finally have a scholarship to offer me and any verbal agreement with Syracuse was meaningless. Two hours later, he was knocking on my parents' door, and after a while he had me convinced." Suffice it to say, Syracuse and Fred Lewis were more than a bit disappointed.

"We were all cocky and could shoot," said Holowaty. "I felt I was better than Wes, but he was a workaholic and so very intelligent." Indeed, had it not been for a severe ankle injury with later leg complications, Holowaty might have been the eventual star.

"As a freshman team, we were so good we felt we could beat our varsity," said Penders (and this was the varsity that later went to the NCAA regional finals). "We had a frosh-varsity game arranged, and we were confident of winning. But it was to be played the night after November 22, 1963, and was of course called off by the death of President Kennedy."

Toby and His Sophomore Pups

In November of 1964 an announcement was made at a home football game that afterward all fans were invited to come into the Field House and watch the upcoming basket-ball team scrimmage. Hundreds flowed in, mainly on word-of-mouth that the 1964–65 team would actually be much better than the team that had beaten Princeton and Bill Bradley only months before.

The center, captain, and soul of the team was senior Toby Kimball. His size and physical strength were matched only by his desire to win. "Toby was a man among boys," Holowaty said. And Shabel knew exactly how to blend his

Wes, Ray, and Rip

Only three players in UConn basketball history have averaged 19 or more points a game, while playing sixty or more career games. Here is how Wes Bialosuknia compares to modern greats Ray Allen and Richard "Rip" Hamilton.

	Games	Total Points	Average Points per Game
Wes Bialosuknia			
1964–65	23	490	21.3
1965–66	24	510	21.3
1966–67	24	673	28.0
Career:	71	1,673	23.6
Ray Allen			
1993–94	34	429	12.6
1994–95	32	675	21.1
1995–96	35	818	23.4
Career:	101	1,922	19.0
Richard "Rip" Hamilton			
1996–97	32	509	15.9
1997–98	37	795	21.5
1998–99	34	732	21.5
Career:	103	2,036	19.8

young sophomores in with his dominant center—the UConn precursor to Emeka Okafor.

Wes Bialosuknia concurs, "All that has been said about Toby is true. He was the man in many ways and simply could not be replaced."

"The only two games we lost that regular season were when Toby was out due to injury, and Wes missed one of those two," said Shabel, implying an undefeated regular season was not out of reach. In December UConn traveled to Boston to take on a highly regarded Boston College team with its legendary coach Bob Cousy. "It was a shoot-out," according to Penders. "Toby refused to let us lose." The 85–81 overtime win was the coming-out party for sophomore Bialosuknia who scored 32 points in the thrilling win. The other memorable regular season game was also an overtime win on the road, this time over Manhattan in the original Madison Square Garden in New York. Kimball blocked a potential game-winning shot at the end of regulation, and Penders sank numerous overtime foul shots to ensure the 80–75 victory in front of by far the largest crowd to watch UConn that year.

UConn finished the regular season at 23 and 2 and ranked fifteenth nationally. It was easily the best team before the arrival of Jim Calhoun. But the NCAA Tournament of that era was a far cry from today's balanced seedings and locations—thus UConn was pitted against number three–ranked St. Joseph's, which was 26 and 1, and the game was to be played at their hometown Palestra. "I called the NCAA to complain, especially since it was the second year in a row we were sent to Philly to play a local team," said Shabel who recalled the 53–48 opening round win against Temple the year before, "but they told me it was not technically St. Joe's home court. I felt I had a strong case since they played all their inner-city Big Five games there."

Yet the first half was all UConn, especially Kimball with a stunning 20 rebounds at the half. Holowaty and

Governor John Dempsey congratulates captain Toby Kimball at the final home game of 1965—at left is sophomore star Wes Bialosuknia and at right is Coach Shabel. (University of Connecticut Archives)

Penders both recall Kimball needing medical treatment for exhaustion in the halftime locker room. "Toby simply ran out of gas from that awesome first half," said Holowaty.

"I was just plain outcoached by Dr. Jack Ramsey," lamented Shabel as to the second half. The Hall of Fame coach from St. Joseph's switched his star guard Matt Goukas in order to stop Bialosuknia, and, said Shabel, "We could not break Wes loose; we had no offense for that."

Thus UConn eventually wilted under both the pressure defense and highly partisan St. Joe's crowd to lose by six. The valiant effort by Kimball in his last UConn game remains vivid in the minds of thousands in Connecticut who watched the grainy black-and-white TV image on Channel 8. Toby's 29 rebounds for the game set a record for the Palestra, which was a showcase arena for college hoops, and it was just enough to give him the nation's rebounding title for that season.

A Controversial Season Ending

With virtually the whole team back except Kimball and the six original Shabel recruits now juniors, hopes remained high for the 1965–66 season. The new center was a reed-slim but highly agile sophomore named Bill Corley, who quickly showed promise. Wes continued his long-range shooting with a 21.3 scoring average—identical to his sophomore year. But the wins were not as easy. By the first of March, there were already seven losses, and a home win was needed over archrival Rhode Island to claim a share of the Yankee Conference title and the chance to again go to the NCAA tourney.

UConn trounced Rhody at Storrs 96–74 to force a one-game playoff to determine which of the cochampions would go to the NCAA. Shabel recalls, "They had me go to tiny Voluntown, halfway between UConn and Rhody, for a coin flip to determine who would host the game. We won the flip, but they still got half the tickets." The resulting UConn tickets were in such demand that many students slept outside the Field House to acquire them.

The playoff game became famous for three reasons: an ejection, a premature TV announcement, and a top-level UConn decision that crushed the players.

Rhode Island was a tough physical team led by an outstanding overall forward named Steve Chubin and a muscular enforcer at center named Art Stephenson. UConn had buried Rhody twice in the prior year, but the Rams were the equal to the Huskies this time around. Tommy Penders, perhaps fifty pounds lighter than Stephenson but who feared no one, took some elbows from the Rhody center early on and soon landed a punch, and the burly Stephenson retaliated. The UConn coach and his player differ on what happened next. "I thought both were thrown out, and for us it was a good trade to get Stephenson out of there," Shabel laughed. However, his point guard is adamant that he remained in. "Fred's wrong—only Stephenson was thrown out, but perhaps we lost because he was stuck with me still playing," said Penders reflecting back in amusement nearly forty years later. Wes Bialosuknia agrees with his backcourt partner, remembering that only Stephenson was thrown out, as his view of the fight was from only 5 feet away.

All seemed to be going UConn's way with some eight minutes to go and the Huskies up by seven points or so. TV announcer Dick Galiette thus said on the air, "If the present Husky lead holds, Channel 8 will be televising UConn's opening NCAA Tournament game." Almost instantly after his words, Rhody took control and won the game 67–62.

Penders clearly recalls the UConn postgame locker room. "We were not that unhappy. Word was that the loser would go to the NIT, and we felt we were good enough to win it. Unlike the loss to St. Joe's a year before in the NCAAs in Philly, we were happy to think we would be at neutral Madison Square Garden, and we felt we could win it all. The NCAA was then always stacked with top powers in the Eastern Regional, so we had a much better chance in the NIT."

Thus when UConn president Homer Babbidge told the team, in the presence of Governor John Dempsey, that UConn had declined the NIT invitation, the players were stunned. Based on a meeting prior to the game, a decision was made at the highest levels of the university that if the team lost, UConn would not go to the NIT. However, neither the players nor Coach Shabel was informed until after the game.

"I played baseball and basketball at a high level all through my youth and college years," Penders recalls, "and being told that we could not go to the NIT was the biggest sports disappointment I ever had. None of us could believe it."

The decision was perhaps one of many that led Fred Shabel to eventually decide to move on from UConn. "Fred Shabel was twenty years ahead of his time in vision and coaching talent," Bill Holowaty remembers. "Had UConn's administration supported him, he would have soon made UConn the Duke of the North."

Wes Bialosuknia said about his UConn coach, "Coach Shabel was a genius. If he had stayed as coach, I'm sure he would have taken teams to the Final Four and maybe won it all once or twice."

The Home Finale against Rutgers

By late 1966 Shabel's great class of six players were all seniors and expectations were extremely high. His first choice was not to appoint a captain. "Wes was of course the star," said Holowaty, "but he was not a leader. I was, as was Tommy, but I think Fred chose not to anoint anyone to keep things balanced."

"I was the point guard, floor leader, and spoke for the team to refs," said Penders. "We had several strong personalities, so it made sense not to choose any one of us."

The early expectations for the season were dampened by two December losses on the road. The Huskies were shocked by losing at Yale, a team with clearly less overall talent. Then UConn was simply outplayed by an excellent Boston College club led by point guard Billy Evans from New Haven. It was an off shooting-night for Bialosuknia, and the BC students started a mocking chant, "What's the matter, Wes?"

But UConn quickly turned matters around by winning ten of its next eleven, though Holowaty still shakes his head at the one loss in that stretch. "We were playing Holy Cross at home," he recalls, "and we had come from behind to tie it late. I am wide open under the hoop at the end of regulation and instead of getting me the ball for an easy hoop, Wes fires a long bomb that misses, and we lose in OT."

But Wes did not misfire often. He set the then single-game scoring record with 50 in a 114–58 rout against Maine. On February 18 at UMass, UConn won a 60–59 thriller to gain at least a share of the Yankee Conference crown. Radio announcer George Ehrlich and WTIC gave

Coach Fred Shabel and his six seniors prior to the memorable home finale against Rutgers. From left to right: Dick Thompson, Bill Holowaty, Ron Ritter, Wes Bialosuknia, P. J. Curran, Tom Penders. (University of Connecticut Archives/Bill Holowaty)

the seniors a 33 rpm record of the final minutes of that key game. Three nights later at home, UConn trounced New Hampshire 114–75 to win the league outright and with it another ticket to the NCAA Tournament. The nets were cut down to celebrate.

That left just one more home game—as good a game as was ever played at the old Field House. The final appearance of the six seniors would have been enough of an attraction, but the opponent was extra special.

Like UConn, Rutgers had become a regional power. Their coach was Bill Foster, who in the late 1970s would take Duke to the NCAA Championship game. Their backcourt was the equal of UConn's with sharpshooting All-America candidate Bobby Lloyd and a point guard, to later attain national coaching renown, named Jim Valvano. Rutgers had been offered an NIT berth, but Coach Foster still had hopes for an NCAA bid, and a win over UConn at Storrs might well achieve that.

The drama was heightened by the race for national scoring champion. The top four scorers in the country were UCLA sophomore Lew Alcindor (later Kareem Abdul-Jabbar), a brilliant senior at Providence named Jimmy Walker, Lloyd of Rutgers, and Wes. In addition, Lloyd had just set an NCAA record for consecutive foul shots made.

Tommy Penders recalls it best by quoting the late Jim Valvano during their later years together in college coaching, when the North Carolina State coach charmed all he met. Regarding that night, February 23, 1967, at Storrs, Valvano recalled:

"Coach Foster broke chalk on the blackboard, he was so pumped up in the pregame. He told us we would never see a crowd like this, but a win over UConn would get us to the NCAA. He told Bobby Lloyd to guard Penders, since Lloyd couldn't guard a chair and Penders would be passing not shooting. Then Coach Foster turns to me, 'You get Wes, and you gotta hold down Wes, no matter what.' We go out on the floor and by the time they do the spotlights and the introductions of the UConn players, the whole damn building is in a frenzy. I'd never seen a crowd like that—at least up until I took my NC State teams to Duke years later.

And then Wes goes nuts shooting, really nuts!!!"

Tommy Penders has a personal video of his times as the backcourt mate to Bialosuknia. "It's loaded with his bombs hitting nothing but the bottom of the net, and that night was the best of them all." By late in the first half, Wes has 27 points, more than the Rutgers team—many of them 25-foot bank shots that would make Celtic great Sam Jones smile. The roof was almost coming off the old Field House.

Penders went on as to his memory of that night. "Fred was a genius of a coach, and he often liked to change defenses. He also was paranoid as to foul trouble. We had a big lead with me guarding Lloyd in the first half, but we go zone in the second half and Lloyd gets on fire. None of us liked to play zone, and we were seeing our lead melt away."

Rutgers made a run at the Huskies; however, it was too little, too late. UConn won 84–77, but the shootout by two of the top four national scorers is the memory that remains. Wes had 40 to Lloyd's 39. Rutgers had to settle for the NIT.

When asked who was better, Lloyd or Bialosuknia, Penders replied, "Oh, Wes—not even close. Lloyd was a standstill shooter who could be guarded, but Wes was much quicker with good moves, especially to his right."

It would be nice to say the era of Shabel, Bialosuknia, and his teammates ended with that last home game, but it did not. UConn went to Rhody on a Saturday afternoon, and Wes put on another shooting clinic as he scored 38. He put UConn up by one with 4 seconds to go, but a buzzer beater gave the Rams an upset win. Wes recalled that long-time UConn sports information director Joe Soltys calculated that for some six hours, Bialosuknia was the nation's leading scorer, until huge scoring nights by Walker and Alcindor.

The regular-season finale was four nights later at Holy Cross, always the nemesis for UConn. It was a totally off night, especially for Wes, resulting in a nine-point loss.

The NCAA opening-round game was a rematch with Boston College, played at Rhode Island's Keaney Gym. The Eagles were loaded with talent, as they had showed in their December win over UConn in Boston. "What people don't remember," said Penders, "is that Bill Corley was hurt the day before the game. He was our inside threat and played only a few minutes." Corley was talented enough to later be drafted for the pros, according to then assistant coach Burr Carlson.

Shabel was candid in saying BC was simply a superior team. "We could not run with them, so I used a strategy which was done on occasion in the ACC (Atlantic Coast Conference). We shortened the game by having Tommy Penders dribble the ball. I was sure they would not change their defense and they didn't. BC coach Bob Cousy was furious with me—he said that sort of slowdown had no place in New England college basketball, but it was our best chance to win."

In those pre–shot clock days, Shabel's strategy almost worked. The score at the half was 14–13, more like a football game. UConn stayed in the game, despite no inside presence and an off shooting-night by Wes, but BC prevailed 48–42. UConn would not see an NCAA game again for another nine years.

An era was over. Fred Shabel never coached another game for UConn, and the six seniors moved on with their lives.

Life after UConn led to major successes for Shabel, Holowaty, and Penders. Shabel went on to become athletic

Shabel, Greer, and Calhoun—and Winning

F red Shabel coached only four seasons at UConn, but his winning percentage holds its own with the two legendary Husky coaches, Hugh Greer and Jim Calhoun.

	Years	Seasons	Won–Lost	Winning Percentage
Hugh Greer	1946–63	17	286–112	.719
Fred Shabel	1963–67	4	72–29	.713
Jim Calhoun	1986–2004	18	432–165	.724

director at Penn in the Ivy League, and he makes clear he never intended to be a long-term head coach. His preference was for management and sports administration. Today he is one of America's top sports executives, as vice chairman of Comcast-Spectacor, which owns the Philadelphia 76ers, the Flyers, and the Wachovia Center.

Bill Holowaty stayed close to Storrs. Soon after UConn he joined Eastern Connecticut State University where he became head baseball coach and has won four national championships in Division III, including one where he coached his son. Still he shakes his head and says, "I've had all these championships here, and still all anybody seems to remember about me is playing on those UConn teams."

Tommy Penders took his lessons learned as Fred Shabel's point guard and turned them into a first-rate college basketball coaching career. Starting at Tufts followed by

Columbia and Fordham, Tommy did battle with the likes of St. John's as fiercely as he fought Rhode Island's Art Stephenson. In 1988 he took an undermanned Rhode Island team to the NCAA Sweet Sixteen, and two years later, he reached the Elite Eight with Texas. He is now the new head coach at the University of Houston, where he gushes over the talent he has and relishes restoring a past power to new collegiate glory.

Wes Bialosuknia was drafted by both the NBA and the then new ABA and signed a three-year guaranteed contract with the Oakland Oaks of the new league. He played one season averaging nine points per game during which he set a record for converting nine three-point shots in a row. That record surprised no one who watched his UConn shooting. Wes was present in 1977 when Tony Hanson broke his record for total points by a Connecticut player, and he was also at the Hartford Civic Center in 2001 to appear at half-time as part of the UConn All-Century Team. With regard to this story, he kindly sent three hand-written letters, from which his quotes are taken. He had nothing but praise for his coach and teammates and added how special his memories are from his Husky career.

To his coach, teammates, and thousands of UConn fans from that period, there is agreement that there was no one quite like Wes. The silent black-and-white footage from the mid-1960s gives proof of not only an all-time UConn star but one of the great shooters ever to wear a college uniform.

Dee Rowe Revives a Winning Tradition

"Six seconds left . . . long pass to Hoagland, down court . . . it's over now . . . he lays it up—and IN . . . **The game is over** *. . . Connecticut has defeated Rhode Island 35 to 32 . . . fans are pouring on the floor and the scene cannot be described over radio."*

—UConn student radio station WHUS play-by-play call by Robert Porter of the end of the memorable "slowdown" win over Rhode Island in 1970

The halftime score was 9 to 7 with UConn trailing its archrival. Yet for the entire half, the fans were on their feet, roaring with passionate support as guards Doug Melody and Bob Staak dribbled away the clock in the days before the shot clock. When the Huskies finally took the lead at 15 to 14 midway through the second half, the crowd was truly deafening.

The UConn Field House was closed for renovation in 1990 when basketball moved to the new Gampel Pavilion. Looking back at the thirty-six seasons played there, the game that most people picked as the number one memory was what has become known as the "slowdown" game. It was the season finale against Rhody and gave UConn a share of the Yankee Conference title with UMass. But that only begins to tell the story.

In the late 1960s UConn basketball had taken a sharp downturn. The 1968–69 team posted a 5 and 19 record after losing its first ten games. Coach Burr Carlson resigned at the end of the season. In addition, the university was adjusting to vast cultural, racial, and political changes, thus basketball seemed far less important than it was only three or four years earlier.

Enter a New England prep school coaching legend, Donald E. "Dee" Rowe, who had created a dynasty at Worcester Academy, where he coached basketball and base-ball. Rowe met the Connecticut media as UConn's new head basketball coach in the fall of 1969. "I come here in hopes of continuing the proud tradition started by Hugh Greer," said Rowe in his opening remarks.

"It's very important to understand the times, the Vietnam years," Rowe said when reflecting on his UConn coaching career. "I really believe that up to then, it was the toughest era to coach in. There was student unrest, including boycotts, strikes, and bomb scares. Much of the atmosphere seemed like anti-God, anti-mother, and anti-country. Students resented authority, and I represented such authority. The black players on my teams were pioneers; no one at the time had any idea of the pressures on them. My real pride was in helping to build lives, and to this day I remain so proud of how my players have led their lives since my coaching days, and watching their success has been a greatest reward."

Rowe's recruitment of black players has been cited as one of his many achievements. His first starting black player, Robert "Bobby" Taylor, recalls with some amusement his coach as an authority figure. "We were on a bus, going to a game I think. The bus stops and Dee announces to the whole team that we will not continue until Taylor visits the barber. I did have quite an Afro in those days, and Coach Rowe had a real hang-up on hair length. I'm sure I argued some, but I did go in, and we compromised on how much was cut," Taylor laughed. "But with my Dad dying in my teens, Dee was as close to a father figure as anyone I had. People do not remember, but when I came to UConn, there were only fifty African Americans on campus. Dee meant the world to me when I played and ever since."

In addition to the off-court challenges, Rowe had to turn around a basketball program that had seemingly lost a winning tradition. It didn't take him long.

The season began with four straight home games. UConn was a slight underdog in its opener with in-state rival Fairfield, and the Huskies were down by six points at the half. However, a late second-half rally and foul shot with 8 seconds to go resulted in a one-point upset win. The next two games were a bit easier with double-digit wins over Yale and New Hampshire.

Next was Boston College, a team that had beaten UConn five straight times over the past four seasons. Like the Huskies, BC had a new head coach. His name was

The Loudest Field House Crowd of All—Three Candidates

Anyone with memories of going to games in the thirty-six years of the Field House can attest to the crowd noise being an enormous advantage for UConn. While Gampel Pavilion is more than twice the size, the Field House acoustics made it sound as loud as any on-campus arena. But which game had the loudest crowd? Here are the three candidates most often mentioned, in chronological order, all being the season home finales for that particular year:

1. 1967 versus Rutgers—the Wes/Lloyd shooting duel. This was the last game played with the original configuration of the Field House. This included seats much closer to the court, a hardwood floor, and nets behind each basket, all of which made the Field House more passionate. The crowd was already enthused due to the final home game for six mainstay seniors. But the volume soon grew much higher due to the incredible long-distance shooting display of Wes Bialosuknia who scored 40 to just edge Rutgers' shooting star Bobby Lloyd who netted 39.

2. 1970 versus Rhode Island—the slowdown game. Bob Staak's memory of crying in pregame warm-ups due to the crowd's passion says it all for this game. The din of sound lasted the full forty minutes, even when nothing more was going on than endless dribbling by Doug Melody and Bob Staak.

3. 1988 versus Virginia Commonwealth—NIT third round. UConn fans were determined to cheer their beloved Huskies right into the NIT Final Four. The crowd was an overflow 4,801, which was a concern to fire marshals. UConn's associate athletic director Tim Tolokan vividly remembers a haze hanging over the floor. He recalled Lynn McCollum who was in charge of facilities saying, "The crowd is making so much noise that they are shaking dust off the rafters."

Picking the loudest of these three is an extremely close call, as opinions are divided, but all agree these were the three best crowds in Field House history.

Chuck Daly, who later had enormous coaching success with two NBA Championships and coached the Olympic gold-medal "dream team" of 1992. As in its opener, UConn again trailed at the half, but a nine-point second-half run led by substitute forward Tom McCrocklin resulted in yet another upset with a 77–72 win.

It was only mid-December, but UConn was just one win away from matching the previous season's victory total. In turn, the season's first road game represented a major challenge. Yankee Conference rival Massachusetts had won the last four games with Connecticut, and its home court, named Curry Hicks Cage, was every bit as tough a place for a visiting team as the UConn Field House. In addition, word-of-mouth quickly spread that UMass had a superstar sophomore named Julius Erving. The game that resulted was, in some ways, more surprising than the far more famous slowdown game of two and a half months later.

Due largely to the inside dominance of UCLA star Lew Alcindor (later Kareem Abdul-Jabbar), the NCAA in the late 1960s had banned the dunk shot from the college game, but it was still allowed in warm-ups. During the pregame warm-ups, the highly partisan UMass crowd became quickly fired up with repeated monster slam dunks by the 6'7" Erving. This, of course, was long before the nickname "Dr. J" was bestowed on the extremely talented forward.

The home court advantage and Erving's instantly obvious skills resulted in UMass scoring the first ten points of the game. Rowe took a time-out to settle his players, and slowly but steadily UConn crept back into the game. It was a one-point game at the half.

UConn cocaptain Ron Hrubala was given the task of covering Erving. "He was good, really good, but then again, I never thought that night that he would become one of the greatest players in basketball history."

The other UConn cocaptain, Bob Staak, had several memories regarding Erving. "I saw him play as a freshman, but that year he was just a nice player to watch, but not *that* good until his sophomore year." Erving was not aggressively recruited from Roosevelt High School on Long Island, but he grew several inches between his freshman and sophomore years.

Through his post-UConn playing and coaching days, Staak came to know Erving and tells one story from the game's second half. "Our point guard Bobby Boyd fed me a terrific backdoor pass just as he was falling down. I was ready to lay the ball in, but there was Erving ready to block it. I somehow managed to go under the hoop and complete a reverse lay-in. I remember that basket being the icing on the cake for our win. As years have gone by, Julius's opinion of me as a player seems to keep rising based on that one basket."

There was plenty of icing to a remarkable cake by the end of this game. UConn was nursing a slight lead with one minute and 26 seconds to go but then ran off the last eleven points of the game to win going away by an 88–71 score. The UMass crowd looked on quietly in disbelief. The reversal of the game's start to its finish was stunning. After falling behind by ten points in the opening minutes, the Huskies had outscored a more talented team on the road by 27 points the rest of the way!! Bob Staak led all players with 22 points, while the sensational Erving had 20. After the dreadful prior season, the Huskies were now 5 and 0 under their new coach. Doug Melody recalled the postgame locker room celebration, "We were exhilarated by the win and were very surprised at having won our first five games."

But the following game epitomized Dee Rowe's emotions during his UConn coaching career. "We go to play at Holy Cross, and we get crushed. As good as I felt winning at UMass, I felt worse by the way we were beaten in my home city of Worcester. Throughout my coaching days, the highs were never as high for me as the lows were devastating."

The loss at Holy Cross in the old Worcester Auditorium was by a score of 122 to 104. The game still holds three all-time UConn records: Most combined points, most points scored by an opponent, and most points in one half by an opponent (69). Guard Bobby Boyd led the Huskies' scoring with 36 points, and Staak had 25 before fouling out with eleven minutes to go. But Connecticut was never really in this game.

The Huskies played roughly .500 for the next two months, winning at times when they were expected to lose and also the opposite. Examples were upsetting Rhode Island on the road 77–74, yet losing at home to a weak Vermont team 69–63.

As the last week of the season began, UConn was 13 and 8. Winning the final two games might lead to a post-season tournament invitation. The next to last game of the year was at Rutgers on a Tuesday night in late February.

Staak was magnificent in a very exciting game, and he recalled it well. "I remember my late-game shooting. I know I had 31 points, but I also recall fouling out on the jump ball for overtime." The Husky press guide for the following season confirms the 31 points and states that Staak had eight long-range field goals in the final six minutes and 15 seconds to lead a UConn comeback and force an overtime. Had the three-point rule been in effect, it would have been an easy Connecticut win as virtually all of those eight shots were from 25 feet or more. For pure long-distance shooting, only Wes Bialosuknia could rival Bob Staak from the 1960s and 1970s UConn era.

But Staak's departure at the start of overtime led to Rutgers taking control, and the Scarlet Knights made all eight of their overtime free throws and won 90 to 84. It was a long and depressing bus ride from central New Jersey back to Storrs that night.

Yet matters would soon turn much worse for the Huskies. Later that week during a practice before the season finale against Rhode Island, state police came to the Field House and led away three key players—top scorer Bobby Boyd, averaging 23.4 points a game, as well as key substitute forwards Tom McCrocklin and Steve Koski. They were under investigation for vending machine break-ins at the UConn ice rink the prior spring. While all three were eventually cleared, there had been a violation of team rules, thus they could not play while pending investigation. The team became depleted even more when, on the day of the game, starting center Tony Budzinsky came down with a temperature of 102 and was too sick to play.

Ron Hrubala recalled the planning before the game. "We were certainly in the David position as compared to Rhode Island as Goliath going into the game. But we did not feel it, as such. Dee Rowe gave us a sense of calm. We

Governor John Dempsey, Coach Rowe and cocaptain Bob Staak before the start of the "slowdown" game against Rhode Island. (University of Connecticut Archives/Dee Rowe)

followed his game plan of holding the ball, and that took away any sense of fear." Rowe gives great credit to his two first-year assistants, Fred Barakat and Dick Stewart, both of whom went on to become head coaches, at Fairfield and Fordham respectively.

Hrubala also remembered how the players differed in their overall approach to basketball in general. "Bob Staak was much more passionate than I was. He made a career out of basketball. I loved to play and played hard, but I was there for an education and had other interests, especially in finance and markets." Hrubala was an outstanding student, as his coach remembered, and Ron turned his UConn education into a successful insurance career in the Hartford area.

Staak was indeed passionate. He recalled the pregame for Rhody as though it were yesterday. "We felt everyone had given up on us after losing so many key players. I really expected the Field House to be only half full. Then we come out for warm-ups and I had never heard anything like the fans and how they were behind us. I actually started crying during the lay-up drill. I never expected anything like that crowd. Then Governor Dempsey joins our huddle just before the opening tip to encourage us even more."

UMass with Erving had beaten the Huskies in the return match at Storrs two weeks earlier and had already won a share of the Yankee Conference title. The winner of the UConn–Rhode Island game would share the crown, and Rhody was a strong team that probably would have been favored even if the Huskies were at full strength.

"I read somewhere that I would have to score 40 for us to have a chance," said Staak. "Instead I take one shot the whole game and miss it. I had all of one point from a foul shot. But Doug Melody and I combined for something like ten assists."

With the careful preparations and pregame fan support, the players took the floor with a sense of confidence, recalled Melody. He added, "We had planned to slow down the game, but probably not to the extent of a 9 to 7 halftime score." With no shot clock and two skilled ball handlers in Staak and Melody, the first half was a standoff, just as Rowe had hoped for.

Taylor recalled the halftime. "We came in the locker room behind, but Coach Rowe was very positive. To me it was strange to be happy when down. But there is no doubt it was the most exciting game I ever played in."

"Our five starters played the whole forty minutes," Staak recalled. "It was Taylor, Doug, Ron, me, and Phil Hoagland." The latter was a little-used substitute center who only scored 65 points the entire season, but 14 of them were in the game of the year.

"Hoagland was not a ball handler," Hrubala said. "We were told to pass to him only when necessary, but he scored by default, and his contribution was crucial."

Well into the second half, a steal by Staak led to a layup by Melody, which put UConn ahead 15 to 14. The crowd by now was in a frenzy of delight and anticipation. Dee Rowe recalled how the game had rallied the campus and the whole state, and the Field House sounded like almost the whole state was in attendance.

The remainder of the game was played at a more normal pace. With 1:22 left, Hoagland scored on a driving layup and was fouled. UConn held a slim lead toward the end, but the game felt far from over, especially due to missed foul shots by the Huskies in the closing minutes.

"We were all exhausted," recalled Melody. "I was even given smelling salts at one point by the team physician, and I still remember missing two key free throws when my shots were short due to fatigue."

Staak remembered the finish. "There were less than ten seconds left, and they score to cut our lead to one, and

UConn's Doug Melody dribbles the clock against Rhode Island. Bob Staak (24) looks on. *(University of Connecticut Archives)*

they are pressing us furiously. Bobby Taylor was to throw the inbound pass and I yell for the ball, expecting Rhode Island to foul me in the backcourt. Instead I see the ball thrown way over my head down court to Hoagland, who has a clear field to the basket." Hoagland's layup at the buzzer made the final score 35 to 32 and set off as wild an on-court celebration as has ever been seen at a Husky home game.

UConn ended the season at 14 and 9 and Yankee Conference cochampions, but without a bid to postseason play. UMass went on to the NIT where Julius Erving first caught the national limelight in a narrow loss to Marquette, which went on to win the tournament.

But the slowdown game transcended any mere win or loss. With the loss of key players due to the investigation, newspaper coverage of UConn basketball went from the sports pages to the front pages. But after the game, the Huskies were the lead story on both.

Dee Rowe was named New England Coach of the Year by his coaching peers and went on to become one of the landmark coaches in Connecticut history. His next two seasons resulted in losing records, but his 1972–73 team, with seven African-American players making major contributions, posted 15 wins, the most since the mid-1960s. His last five seasons, with Dom Perno as his top assistant, all produced winning records. Dee always felt that Dom shared equally in the success of that era. The combined record was 88–48, with standout years of 19–8 in 1973–74 and 19–10 in 1975–76.

"But I became a burnout," Rowe reflected. "I developed too many medical problems, and the highs did not make up for the lows. I finally decided to make my family Hertz instead of Avis, so I stopped coaching at age forty-eight. I was the oldest coach in Division I in New England at the time." Thanks to the vision of athletics director John Toner, Rowe was made the first Associate Director of Athletics for Development, and thus the new University of Connecticut Athletics Development Fund was created. It was the first official athletic fund-raising position in New England.

Today, more than thirty-five years after the slowdown game, Dee Rowe remains active at UConn as special adviser for athletics, after many years of service as associate director of athletics for development. Dee is beloved by all

Dee Rowe's Best Team

When asked which team was his best, Dee Rowe said, "We had a great team in 1973–74 when we upset St. John's in the NIT in Madison Square Garden. Super senior guard Jimmy Foster led the way with 27 points and was named All-NIT. However, the 1975–76 team, with the thrilling way we ended the season, had to be the best."

This choice was validated by the last four games, all played in March of 1976. In the days before the Big East Conference, the top four teams in New England met to play for an NCAA berth as the ECAC New England Champion. UConn first upset top-seeded UMass in the Springfield Civic Center. That set up a match with Providence, coached by highly respected Dave Gavitt, who had been an assistant to Rowe years earlier at Worcester Academy. Connecticut raced to a large early lead over the heavily favored Friars and won the New England Championship with an 87–73 victory. Junior forward Tony Hanson, the outstanding player of the Rowe era, had a brilliant year averaging 19.1 points per game and was selected New England Player of the Year as a senior. Another star from the 1975–76 team was center John Thomas, who was named New England Player of the Year for that season. The excellent guard play from Joey Whelton and Al Weston also made huge contributions, while freshmen Jim Abromaitis and Randy LaVigne were strong in reserve roles.

Tony Hanson (left) was the best player in the Dee Rowe (right) era.
(University of Connecticut Division of Athletics)

In their NCAA opener, the Huskies trailed Hofstra by 13 at the
half. But Connecticut rallied to force overtime and won 80–78. Jeff
Carr led the team with 17 points and 15 rebounds. It was UConn's
first NCAA game in nine seasons and its first NCAA win in twelve
years. The season ended with a 93–79 loss to then undefeated
Rutgers in the NCAA Sweet Sixteen in Greensboro Coliseum in North
Carolina.

who have ever known him personally, and his coaching skills are still widely praised. "I learned a lot from Dee, and his stack offense was very innovative," said Jim Calhoun. Such nationally recognized coaches as Dave Gavitt and Jim Valvano were assistants to Dee in his long career, as were many major UConn names such as Dom Perno and Bob Staak.

Dee Rowe was "UConn's ambassador"—a direct quote from his most successful protégé, Dave Gavitt. "This was especially true after he left active coaching but stayed at Connecticut. Dee was the guy most people would contact concerning UConn athletics, and he has represented the university superbly."

Former coaching rival at both Dartmouth and Holy Cross and present assistant coach George Blaney has similar sentiments. "Dee was so passionate about basketball it almost killed him physically. In turn, he was a teacher first and foremost. Once you became his friend, it was for life. He believes totally in doing the right thing and doing as much as you can for other people."

But when he looks back on the slowdown game, Dee just smiles and says, "I should have quit right there and then after that game." It was the ultimate high for him and his players, as well as a unifying moment of joy for the state of Connecticut.

Enter into the Bright Lights

W hat was the single most significant reason Connecticut basketball evolved from a midlevel regional program into a national powerhouse? In other words, what created the "Beast of the East," as displayed on many T-shirts over the past fifteen years? Certainly, Jim Calhoun coming to Storrs in 1986 had an impact that cannot be overestimated. Also, the opening of a first-rate on-campus arena in Gampel Pavilion in 1990 was huge. But years before, a decision was made that affected all that would follow for Husky basketball. Without the politics that created the Big East Conference, UConn would not be the force it is today in college basketball.

The explosion that led to UConn's national prominence began with a match lit by a very unlikely source. John Toner, UConn's athletics director for twenty years from 1968 to 1988, retains a razor sharp memory at age eighty-one. He recalled the following:

"The Eastern College Athletic Conference (ECAC) was and still is an invaluable service organization to more than 200 colleges, including eligibility rules and officiating for up to thirty intercollegiate sports. In the mid-1970s, the ECAC provided four regional qualifying tournaments to determine NCAA representatives from the East, with Region One being New England."

Since the Yankee Conference and Ivy League had lost their automatic NCAA qualifying status, the four-team post-season ECAC New England Tournament had drawn considerable interest since its 1975 inception. With the ECAC as a holding company of sorts, major New England teams could play whom they liked in the regular season and an ECAC tournament committee would choose the four who would play for the automatic NCAA berth.

But Toner also recalled a concerned New England athletics director. As the present AD at Ohio State, Andy Geiger is now one of the most powerful men in college sports. In the late 1970s he was the AD at Brown. Since Ivy League rules prevented its members from any post-season play except for the NCAA itself, Geiger was challenged. He thus put forth legislation within the NCAA that, if passed, would require conferences to have single round-robin play with a postseason tournament or double round-robin (home and home) without a conference postseason tournament in order to have a bid to the NCAA Tournament. Since this was certain to be passed, it spelled doom for events such as the ECAC New England Tournament, and it proved to be the catalyst for forming new conferences.

Geiger, who would later win the annual College Football Hall of Fame award in John Toner's name for outstanding administrative contributions, had created a problem for New England's most successful college coach of the 1970s. Dave Gavitt was justifiably proud of his Providence College Friars who had been to the NCAA Tournament in 1972, '73, '74, '77, and '78, with his 1973 team making it to the Final Four. Gavitt, a creative and forward thinker, saw the likely end of the four-team ECAC New England Tournament as affecting the future for basketball at Providence.

"It was the fall of 1978," Gavitt recalled, "and the pending change might require us to play teams such as Maine and New Hampshire twice a year, and that was not how we wanted to go. So my thinking was to look into a potential new league or be a pure independent."

"In considering a new league, I sought out two great coaches in Louie Carnesecca at St. John's and John Thompson at Georgetown," said Gavitt. "Louie wasn't sure—he had a good thing going with the status quo, but John indicated to me that if I could pull it off Georgetown was interested."

"I next sought out my college classmate from Dartmouth, Jake Crouthamel, who was the AD at Syracuse. They were interested, so our four colleges met many times in the next few months."

"Our approach was to touch every major East Coast market plus the hotbeds, and we at Providence were a hotbed and Syracuse certainly was one. We wanted a second team from the New York market, and Seton Hall fit nicely by moving into the Meadowlands Arena. Philly was important to us, and this led to complications."

The complication arose due to a newly formed conference then known as the Eastern Eight. This conference was

The Big East and Its Impact on New England

From the mid-1950s to the late 1970s, New England college basketball was a close-knit group of six colleges with winning traditions. Three joined the Big East Conference as charter members, while the other three went separate ways. The NCAA Tournament is the widely acknowledged barometer of college basketball excellence, in both appearances and how far a team advances. The table on page 65 shows the impact of Big East membership and NCAA success over the twenty-five seasons of the conference to date, 1980 through 2004.

the precursor to today's Atlantic 10 Conference. Its 1978 membership had a strong football flavor with Penn State, Pittsburgh, Rutgers, and West Virginia. The other members at that time were Duquesne, George Washington, Massachusetts, and Villanova. As it turned out, Rutgers decided not to entertain serious discussions with the founders of what was to become known as the Big East, due to their football priorities. The same was true for Temple, an independent at that time. However, Villanova said it would join after a one-year delay, in order to smoothly exit the Eastern Eight. Thus the Philadelphia market was included.

New England, specifically the Boston area, became much more complex. Dave Gavitt remembered the views of his committed non–New England members. "They did not

College	Appearances	Won–Lost	Regional Finals	Final Fours	Championships
Non-Big East					
Holy Cross	5	0–5	0	0	0
Massachusetts	7	11–7	2	1	0
Rhode Island	5	6–5	1	0	0
Big East					
Boston College	10	15–10	2	0	0
Providence	7	7–7	2	1	0
CONNECTICUT	12	34–10	6	2	2

want New England to be the Tobacco Road of the new league." (This was a reference to the four closely situated North Carolina members of the Atlantic Coast Conference.) "Thus the message to me was, more or less, to limit New England members to a maximum of three, and since we at Providence were already in, that meant only two more."

"We thought at first that Holy Cross was the strongest New England choice," Gavitt said, "and coach George Blaney and athletic director Ron Perry Sr. were definitely in favor, but Holy Cross president Father John Brooks seemed to have doubts."

Gavitt recalled, "Holy Cross never formally turned us down, but their hesitation led us to speak to Boston College."

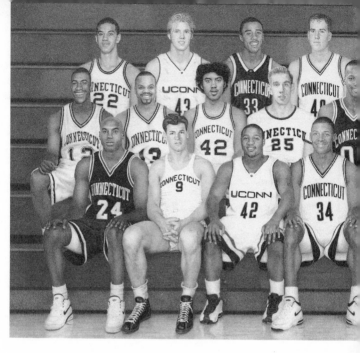

"Yes, we were asked," recalled George Blaney, who was head coach at Holy Cross for twenty-two years and is presently a UConn assistant under Jim Calhoun. "Some of us were not crazy about the idea, but we saw for sure the problems ahead if we did not go." Blaney added, "Staying out did not affect us at Holy Cross at first. The school most immediately affected was Rutgers."

All agreed the discussions were intense among the close-knit New England college basketball fraternity. John Toner, whose discussions were at the athletics director and university president level, was clear regarding loyalties. "Boston College and Holy Cross were very concerned about each other, just as we at UConn were connected to Rhode Island. UMass had already cast their lot with the Eastern Eight so we felt no commitment to them, but I

This drawing of the UConn All-Century Team by Lee Kasai turned back the clock for older players and placed younger players among legends. (University of Connecticut Division of Athletics)

cared deeply about Rhode Island and its AD Maurice 'Moe' Zarchen."

Gavitt, Blaney, and Toner have slightly differing recollections as to the certainty of UConn being included in the original Big East membership.

"I was strong on UConn being included," Gavitt said, "but it was hard convincing some others. I told everyone Connecticut was not only a hotbed but a sleeping giant." But could UConn have been left out had Holy Cross said a quick "yes" on the condition Boston College also be asked? Given the urging of several influential schools that New

England be limited to three members, Dave Gavitt was hesitant to give a firm reply to the hypothetical question. But it never evolved that way.

George Blaney said, "UConn was getting in, no matter what. We all knew UConn really was a sleeping giant. Plus, Dave really wanted them, and his powers of persuasion were enormous."

Toner also felt UConn would get in, but one key issue was the strong tradition with Rhode Island and his own loyalty to Moe Zarchen. "Dave Gavitt had to make this final, and so BC and we were given twenty-four hours to say 'yes' or 'no'—and others were waiting if we said 'no.' BC athletics director Bill Flynn got a green light from Holy Cross to go, so he said an instant yes to Gavitt. I had to do the same with Moe at Rhody. I actually woke him up early that Sunday morning, and I recall he was groggy. Even when less than alert, Moe was a gentleman and saw the reality and told me to go ahead." Toner recalled that Rhode Island did have hard feelings about being left out.

Thus the new conference announced its membership in 1978 with seven charter members: Boston College, Connecticut, Georgetown, Providence, St. John's, Seton Hall, and Syracuse, with insiders aware that Villanova would be the eighth team just a year later. "The new league started with a great public relations move," John Toner said. "The ECAC had a TV contract running through 1979 and needed the money. The Big East allowed that contract to be completed, and those of us close to the ECAC never forgot that."

Since a few of the coaches had expressed doubts that UConn could compete at the level of the other conference members, the challenge of doing well on the court was immediate.

UConn's coach at the time, Dom Perno, remembers the feeling clearly. "We knew if we lacked a total long-term commitment to upgrade, it would be a problem. For example, we loved the Field House on game nights, but we also knew it had aged and could not compare to other facilities we were competing against. One time we had to divert a recruit from seeing the Field House due to a leaking roof."

Perno continued, "We had a great team to start play in the Big East. My best team was the prior year when we won twenty-one games and the ECAC New England Championship and lost a close NCAA game to Syracuse." UConn entered the new league with top players such as Corny Thompson and Mike McKay, both just sophomores as Big East play began.

UConn was indeed very competitive for the first three seasons of Big East competition. The Huskies were 3 and 3 in single round-robin play in the inaugural season of 1979–80 and went 8 and 6 in the league the following year, with that 1980–81 team being the third straight to post 20 or more total wins.

It was the next season, 1981–82, that provided the reality check of just how tough UConn's new league was. The January highlight had been an upset win at Georgetown. The Hoyas were led by star freshman center Patrick Ewing, the best player UConn had faced since Julius Erving more than a decade before. John Toner recalls the night. "It turned out to be the last home game ever for Georgetown in their McDonough on-campus arena. Our sophomore guard Karl Hobbs had been a high school teammate of Ewing's in

Cambridge, Massachusetts. I remember Hobbs making a stunning dribble under the legs of Georgetown star Sleepy Floyd and then scoring what proved to be the key basket." UConn won the game 63–52. Hobbs later became a UConn assistant coach under Jim Calhoun and is currently the head coach at George Washington University.

In the first week of February of 1982, the Huskies won on the road over New England Big East rivals Providence and Boston College. The former was an overtime win, and the latter put Connecticut in first place in league play with a 6 and 2 record. Winning at BC's raucous Roberts Center was never an easy task, and that Boston College team would later make it all the way to the NCAA Midwest Regional Final.

But then it all fell apart for UConn. The Huskies would lose five of their last six regular-season games, all in league play and two in overtime. So instead of finishing as a top seed or nearly so for the Big East Tournament, Connecticut was a sixth seed in the league and matched against number-three seed St. John's.

In its first three years, the league rotated its postseason tournament, prior to establishing Madison Square Garden as the permanent venue in 1983. The third Big East Tournament was held in the Hartford Civic Center, which had been renovated and expanded since the collapse of its roof only hours after a January 1978 UConn home game there.

With a highly partisan UConn crowd behind them, the Huskies and St. John's fought a close, defensive struggle. With the game tied in the closing seconds, St. John's freshman sharpshooter Chris Mullin took a deep corner shot that hit nothing but the bottom of the net, and St. John's won 54–52.

All-time Starting Five, Pre–Jim Calhoun

I n the more than thirty years between the mid-1950s and Jim Calhoun's 1986 arrival at UConn, there were many star players. A survey of a wide range of long-time Husky observers came up with a consensus of an all-time starting five from those years, listed below in chronological order:

Art Quimby, 1951–55 (twice led nation in rebounding; career rebound average of 21.5; career scoring average of 17.5)

Toby Kimball, 1962–65 (led nation in rebounding in 1964–65 with 21.0 average; career rebound average of 17.9; career scoring average of 18.4)

Wes Bialosuknia, 1964–67 (still UConn's all-time scoring leader in career points per game at 23.6 and single-season points per game at 28.0; second highest single-game scoring of 50 points; UConn's all-time leading scorer in total points when his career ended)

Tony Hanson, 1973–77 (four-year starter with 111 games played; career scoring average of 17.9; career scoring total of 1,990 points broke Bialosuknia's then career scoring total record; presently third leading all-time scorer in UConn history)

Corny Thompson, 1978–82 (four-season starter with 114 games played; all-time leader in career free throws made; fifth in career rebounds; fifth in career scoring)

"That shot was a dagger to us," Dom Perno recalled. "Yes, it was the worst loss of my UConn coaching career, though the overtime NIT loss at Dayton six nights later was just about as tough."

Looking back, the Mullin shot in Hartford was the precursor to a difficult era for UConn in arguably the nation's best basketball conference in the 1980s. The 1982 Georgetown team with Ewing lost a one-point NCAA Championship game to North Carolina but returned to the Final Four in 1984 and won it all. Then in 1985 the six-year-old Big East Conference did something never achieved before or since. It placed three of its teams in the Final Four, with Villanova upsetting Georgetown to claim the title.

However, for UConn the five-year span from 1982 through 1987 saw losing seasons. Some UConn supporters started to raise doubts that others had in the late 1970s, regarding the Huskies' ability to compete at such a high level.

But help was on the way. On his last day as UConn athletics director in 1988, John Toner took a shovel in hand and broke ground for the new on-campus basketball facility to be known as the Harry A. Gampel Pavilion.

While the doubters of the late 1970s and mid-1980s had their moment, the original term of "sleeping giant" used by both Gavitt of Providence and Blaney of Holy Cross proved to be the most prophetic. It took some time, but when that giant in Storrs awoke, college basketball had a new superpower.

Of course a man named Calhoun had a lot to do with that, but so did two men of foresight years earlier. They were John Toner and Dave Gavitt, whose combined efforts brought UConn into the bright lights.

A Man from Boston Takes Over

John Toner recalled a habit he formed during his twenty years as UConn athletics director. "I liked to sit at the left corner of the scorer's table for basketball home games, so I could get a close-up view of the visiting coach." Toner had just such a view on December 28, 1985, as it was Huskies against Huskies at the Hartford Civic Center in the Connecticut Mutual Classic. The visiting team was the Northeastern Huskies, coached by Jim Calhoun, and they upset UConn by a score of 90–73 in the championship game.

"I saw how intently the Northeastern players listened to their coach, how hard they played, and what good shape they were in at the end of the game," said Toner. "With Northeastern, Calhoun often could only recruit second or third level players, but he used excellent coaching and better conditioning to get the most out of them."

Toner remembered all that just months later when UConn coach Dom Perno resigned after the 1985–86 season. He knew someone with energy, drive, and coaching talent would be needed to turn around a program with four consecutive losing seasons.

Calhoun vividly remembers the recruitment process. "I was one of three finalists. The others were Mitch Buonaguro, the head coach at Fairfield, who was coming off a twenty-five-win season, and Nick Macarchuk from Canisius." Howie Dickenman, a UConn assistant coach the prior four years, was a man hopeful of being retained. He recalls the same three names, feeling that his chances of staying at UConn were good with two of those candidates.

But Toner, the main decision-maker, gives a different version. "There really was no other candidate in my mind aside from Jim. I knew he might not take it, so I needed a backup choice, but Jim was really the only one in my mind." Toner's backup plan was successful Holy Cross coach George Blaney, a man Toner greatly respected and who today serves as a key assistant to Calhoun on the Husky coaching staff. But if choosing Jim Calhoun was easy, convincing him to come to Connecticut was not.

"John Toner met me at the halfway place between Boston and UConn, a place called the Oxbow Inn in Sturbridge," said Calhoun, "and he asked me what it would take for me to say yes. Well, I was already a tenured professor at Northeastern, all my family roots were in the Boston area, I was promised the athletics directorship at Northeastern when I wanted to get out of coaching, we had just been to five of the last six NCAA Tournaments, I had my best-ever team coming back, I had just turned down Northwestern from the Big Ten, and I was really not in the mood to go anywhere."

But there seems to have been a combination of reasons he finally said yes to UConn.

Calhoun's coaching win over Connecticut in late 1985 was far from his first memory of UConn basketball. "As a young player, my coach Bill Callahan brought me to the UConn Field House to get a sense of big-time New England basketball. It had a special romantic atmosphere."

Later, Calhoun saw the Field House while a star player for Division II American International College. For nearly two decades AIC was the traditional opening game for UConn, and Calhoun played against some very good Connecticut teams led by Husky star Toby Kimball. The record book shows Calhoun once scored 27 against UConn, and Kimball joked that probably many were off of him.

"UConn opened our new building, named the Butova Gym, and we were appreciative of that," Calhoun said. The date was December 1, 1965, and AIC was competitive in an 89–72 loss. "Our freshman team had beaten UConn, so we were no longer the easy opening game, and the series was soon ended by Connecticut." Jim Calhoun was named a Division II All-American and had a tryout with the Celtics.

It is easy to understand why Toner chose Calhoun, who had taken Northeastern to exceptional success, especially in the 1980s. In the 1982 NCAA Tournament, Northeastern won its opening game over St. Joseph's and then lost a true classic—a triple-overtime 76–72 loss to Villanova. Before UConn approached him, Calhoun had taken his teams to the NCAAs three straight years and five of the previous six.

Telling the story of why he finally said yes, Calhoun mentioned the influence of former Husky head coach Dee Rowe, a common thread in much of UConn's basketball history. "I recall the old New England basketball clinics for coaches at Pleasant Valley in Massachusetts where Dee

The Bite of Jim Calhoun's Huskies—from Northeastern

By the time John Toner asked Jim Calhoun what it would take for him to say yes to UConn, Calhoun had developed a powerhouse in Boston at Northeastern. His coaching skill was immediately obvious with a 19–7 record in his first year of 1972–73. But it was in the 1980s that Northeastern under Calhoun became an NCAA regular with five appearances and three upset wins as follows:

Year of NCAA Appearance	Opponent	Score
1981	Fresno State	Won 55–53
	Utah	Lost 94–69
1982	St. Joseph's	Won 63–62
	Villanova	Lost 76–72 (3 overtimes)
1984	Long Island University	Won 90–87
	Virginia Commonwealth	Lost 70–69
1985	Illinois	Lost 76–57
1986	Oklahoma	Lost 80–74

would speak. He was my mentor and friend. He spent several hours with me talking about UConn. He told me that for the right person, this can be a very special place. He introduced me to UConn president Harry Hartley, and we also spent a lot of time in the car just talking of what UConn was about."

Another factor that influenced Calhoun was the UConn campus. "I took a walk around it by myself," he said. "I liked it being self-enclosed and yet in a good location with access to other places. I saw things about UConn that others did not know they had here. There was the great tradition of regional basketball and the very good base of Connecticut high school players."

Finally, there was also the sharp contrast between the Boston and Connecticut markets. Calhoun was at Northeastern when the famous NBA and college coach Rick Pitino was coaching at Boston University. "We joked with each other that we were competing to be the tenth sports story in a nine-story town, given the Red Sox, Bruins, Harvard, Boston College, and so much else." In a 1994 interview on Boston television with WBZ's Bob Lobel prior to a game at Boston College, Calhoun was asked why he left the Boston area for Connecticut. He replied, "Well, one reason is that tonight nearly half of the television sets in Connecticut will be turned on to our game."

Ten years later, the passion of Husky fans has only grown. Calhoun illustrated this with a story from the summer of 2004. "I'm playing golf at Coyote Moon Golf Course out near Lake Tahoe, and by noon that is posted on the UConn Boneyard." (The Boneyard is an Internet discussion forum devoted to Husky fanatics at www.uconnfan.com.) Calhoun made it clear he has never visited the Boneyard.

Then UConn assistant coach Howie Dickenman described the last-minute drama surrounding Calhoun's final decision. "I knew Jim had been offered the job, and if he took it, I was hopeful he would retain me as an assistant. The decision day comes and I am in touch with Karl Fogel,

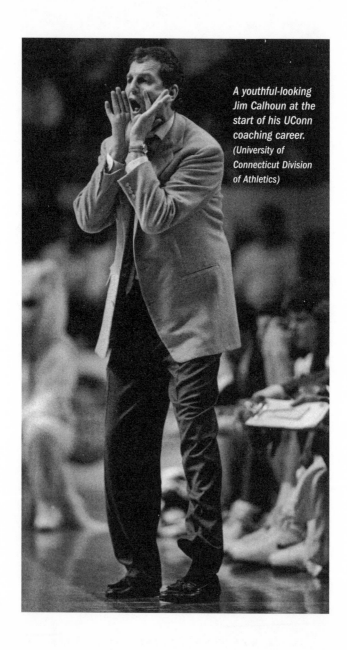

A youthful-looking Jim Calhoun at the start of his UConn coaching career. (University of Connecticut Division of Athletics)

an assistant coach at Northeastern. He tells me Calhoun has asked for another thirty minutes before giving his answer. I am in regular touch with my wife, since my own future might be at stake. Finally, I'm called again and told he has said yes to UConn."

As he had hoped, Dickenman was asked to stay on and work for Calhoun. They went over the roster of returning players, analyzing their skills and statistics. "They were pictured on a bulletin board, and I went through all seven returning players. Jim listened to me and replied, 'is that all?'"

Dickenman also recalls another moment in Calhoun's first days at Storrs. "We are walking down the back stairs in the Field House, and Jim tells me something is missing. I asked what did he mean, and he says, 'I don't hear any sound of basketballs bouncing on the court by players practicing—that tells me something is missing and needs to change.'" Dickenman added that the very next day the sounds of many basketballs could be heard on the practice floors.

But the Jim Calhoun coaching era at Connecticut did not have an auspicious start. Dickenman remembered being away on a recruiting trip and missing the opening home exhibition game against an Australian team. "I phone back to find out how we did, and Jim tells me we lost and that some Husky fans started chanting, 'We want Dom,'" in reference to the recently resigned coach Dom Perno.

The regular season did not start smoothly either. Calhoun's first coaching victory at UConn was a 58–54 season-opening win over UMass at the Field House. Senior Gerry Besselink had 18 points and 15 rebounds for the Huskies. But three nights later, UConn was upset by Yale in overtime 77–75, in New Haven. "All of us were taken into the Field House after the return to campus," Dickenman said, "and we got our first real tongue lashing that night—it must have gone on until 2:00 A.M."

The long-time Husky assistant coach went on to make a key observation about the man he worked with for ten seasons. "Jim was a bad loser—and he could be a bad winner too, if we had somehow won while playing badly. I remember us winning up at Holy Cross by a point on a game-ending basket by Steve Pikiell. I say congratulations to Jim and he replies, 'For what?' He was like that not only to motivate us but to motivate himself."

Later in that first month, an overtime game went the Huskies' way, with a 96–94 win over traditional rival Rhode Island. "I remember that game pretty well," said Besselink, the standout big man that year. "I think I had something like 22 rebounds, and I remember how good Coach Dickenman was with the big men like me." Besselink, a Canadian from Kingston, Ontario, was indeed a bright spot in an otherwise rugged year. He averaged a double-double in points and rebounds for the season and in Big East games, with no other Husky achieving this under Calhoun until Emeka Okafor sixteen seasons later.

While Calhoun had expressed concern over the talent level to Dickenman months earlier, two sophomores—Cliff Robinson and Phil Gamble—were showing promise. Sixteen games into the season, UConn was 6–10, but Robinson was averaging 18.1 points per game, and Gamble's scoring average was 11.1. Then in late January 1986, both were declared academically ineligible, and an already undermanned team was severely weakened.

Calhoun surveys the action. Long-time assistant coach Howie Dickenman (left) is behind him.
(University of Connecticut Division of Athletics)

Dickenman remembered the season's definitive win. "We had just lost Cliff and Phil, and we go up to Boston College to play them in the Boston Garden. We gutted out that win. We had no business being on the same floor with them, as we had taken walk-on players as replacements." The 66–60 upset of BC was an early indicator of Calhoun's long-term success over the Big East team from his home city.

But the lack of talent soon took its toll. In the mid-1980s, the Big East was the nation's preeminent college basketball conference. Georgetown had made the Final Four three times with superstar center Patrick Ewing, winning the championship in 1984. In 1985 the league had three of the Final Four teams with St. John's, Villanova, and Georgetown. The Wildcats upset the Hoyas 66–64 in an all–Big East National Championship game.

The depleted 1986–87 UConn team simply could not keep pace with the rest of the league. Following the upset win in Boston, the Huskies lost nine of their final eleven games. The only bright moment was a rousing final home game send-off for Besselink with a tight 56–54 win over Seton Hall at the Hartford Civic Center. Besselink, who played for the Canadian national team, recalled how vigorous Calhoun was in the one season he played for him. Gerry later played in Finland and now lives there with his Finnish wife and their children. He has remained close to UConn over the years and participated in both Jim Calhoun UConn Alumni Charity Games.

Calhoun's debut season at UConn ended with a first-round loss to Boston College in the Big East Tournament by a score of 61–59. The final record was 9 wins and 19 losses; yet given the talent level and the midseason loss of two top players, even nine wins could be seen as over-achieving.

But the record left an imprint on the first-year coach that would not soon be forgotten. One example was that steps were taken to provide a thorough classroom support system for players to prevent further losses of players due to academics.

When asked to give a memory from the end of Calhoun's first season, Howie Dickenman recalled a vivid quote. "Jim told me 'We will never, *ever* experience a season like this again.'"

Time has shown that prediction to be correct, just as time has validated John Toner's observations of opposing coaches from the left corner of the scorer's table.

That First Sweet Taste—The 1988 NIT

A sk any long-time UConn fan to name the first turning point in the Huskies ascension from a regional to a national program, or ask that same fan the most surprising postseason accomplishment in Connecticut basketball history. The reply will likely be the same. It was the totally unexpected surge to the 1988 NIT title, the first national crown of any sort won by UConn basketball.

Jim Calhoun said winning the NIT Championship was the third greatest moment in his UConn coaching career, behind the two NCAA titles. Yet he implies being third underrates what the NIT did for the program. "The NIT win became the world for us," he recalled. "It was a wake-up call that we were for real."

Calhoun continued, "UConn had had five straight losing seasons, including my first, and if we had not done anything in my first four or so seasons, a losing mentality would have set in. We had to give our fans something. You had to be there, on the floor in Madison Square Garden to see the [13,799] fans storming the floor when we won. For that moment in time, it was as exciting as 1999 [his first NCAA Championship] or 2004 [his second]. It really was as meaningful at the time, as 1999 or 2004."

The Madison Square Garden–based NIT began in 1938, a year before the first NCAA Tournament. In the 1950s, it was regarded as the better of the tournaments, according to UConn's Worthy Patterson, a star player from that era. The Huskies first appeared in the 1955 NIT, losing a first-round shoot-out to St. Louis 110–103. In 1966, UConn players were devastated to learn the university had turned down an NIT bid, since they badly wanted to play in the New York limelight. In 1974 Dee Rowe led one of his best teams to a major NIT first-round upset over St. John's on the fabled Garden floor before losing in the quarterfinals to Boston College. UConn returned to the NIT in 1975 but lost in the first round to South Carolina.

But a short time later, the oldest national college basketball postseason tournament made major changes. In 1977 the field remained at sixteen teams, but opening-round games were played outside New York, on the home courts of selected teams. By the following year only the final four teams were making the trip to New York to play the semifinals and finals in Madison Square Garden. In 1979 the field was expanded to twenty-four teams, and in 1980 it expanded again to thirty-two total teams.

For UConn the enlarged NIT with the new venues for early-round games resulted in appearances in 1980, 1981, and 1982. The only victory, however, was in 1981, when a first-round win over South Florida in Tampa was followed by a second-round loss to Minnesota in Hartford. The

Golden Gophers were led by sharpshooter Trent Tucker who scored 35 points, shooting a stunning 14 for 17 from the floor in an 84–66 win. In the prior year (1980) Connecticut had lost in the Field House to St. Peters 71–56, and the 1982 team lost a heartbreaking 76–75 overtime game to Dayton at their arena in Ohio. That March 10, 1982, loss was remembered by former coach Dom Perno as one of the most painful defeats in his UConn coaching career.

Thus, prior to the invitation on Sunday night, March 13, 1988, UConn had appeared in six NIT Tournaments, with only two wins in eight games.

It was far from a sure thing that UConn would even be included in the thirty-two-team 1988 NIT field. While much improved over the 9 and 19 record of Jim Calhoun's initial season the year before, the 1987–88 regular season was barely above the .500 mark at 14 and 13. Even with that improvement, the Huskies were still often overmatched within Big East play, with a league record of 4 wins and 12 defeats, losing their last four conference games in February to Syracuse, Boston College, Pittsburgh, and St. John's.

This meant the Huskies were forced into the dreaded eight versus nine game in the annual Big East Tournament as the lowest seed, playing number eight seed Providence. UConn defeated the Friars 75–62 for its first Big East Tournament win in eight years and only its second league-tournament win ever. As expected UConn lost the next game to top seed Pittsburgh 75–58, but when the Huskies walked off the Madison Square Garden floor after that loss, only the wildest dreamer could imagine the celebration that would take place on the same court just nineteen days later.

Assistant coach Howie Dickenman recalls that Sunday night when the phone rang. "We were led to believe we would be invited, and we had hopes of even getting a home game. We knew Dave Gavitt (Big East commissioner) was pushing for us, but it was a surprise to learn we were going to have to go down and play at West Virginia."

Connecticut had not played West Virginia since losing to them 77–71 in the NCAA Tournament twenty-five years earlier. The Huskies' NIT visit to Morgantown was seven years before the Mountaineers joined the Big East Conference as a basketball member in 1995.

Dickenman collected an inspirational souvenir from UConn's hotel. "It was the Lakeview Resort and Conference Center, and I found something that said, 'Encourage your hopes, not your fears.' I still have that with me today."

Second-year guard Steve Pikiell had a different sort of memory from the visit to West Virginia. "Just as we come out on the court, they shoot off a musket with a sound so loud that it was scary. We struggled from the get-go, and it was such a grind-it-out game."

Jim Calhoun has a vivid memory of the hoop that turned the UConn program around. When asked if Tate George's game-tying basket with 6 seconds left in regulation was his most important shot for UConn, Calhoun replies, "It's not even close. The famous shot Tate took at the buzzer to beat Clemson in the 1990 NCAA was a national story and one of the great NCAA finishes, so it was nice. But the greatest shot Tate George ever took was a bank jump shot coming down the lane, which allowed us to win at West Virginia and in turn allowed us to later win the third most significant win in my years here at Connecticut."

A Historical Quirk—UConn, the NIT, and Presidential Inaugurals

Since winning the 1988 NIT title, UConn basketball postseason has had a little-known parallel to American politics. In every season that has included a presidential inauguration in January, from 1989 through 2004, UConn has played in the NIT, while in all other seasons, the Huskies have made it to their goal of the NCAA Tournament. The record is as follows:

Season	Presidential Inaugural	UConn post-season result
1988–89	George H. W. Bush	NIT (3rd round)
1989–90	none	NCAA
1990–91	none	NCAA
1991–92	none	NCAA
1992–93	Bill Clinton	NIT (1st round)
1993–94	none	NCAA
1994–95	none	NCAA
1995–96	none	NCAA
1996–97	Bill Clinton	NIT (3rd place)
1997–98	none	NCAA
1998–99	none	NCAA Champions
1999–00	none	NCAA
2000–01	George W. Bush	NIT (2nd round)
2001–02	none	NCAA
2002–03	none	NCAA
2003–04	none	NCAA Champions

West Virginia missed a free throw with 33 seconds left, and after a deflection, George had to leap to catch the inbounds pass. He then used a high screen from Jeff King and hit the 6-foot running shot that sent the game into overtime.

Pikiell and Dickenman both recall how the sophomore George carried the team in the closing minutes of this crucial game. Pikiell said Tate really took over the last four minutes, and Dickenman recalled how underappreciated his rebounding was down the stretch. "We were just so glad to get out of there," Pikiell said, "we were a team of grinders and nothing came easily for us." George led UConn with 15 points, adding 9 assists and 6 rebounds.

George's shot at West Virginia triggered what former coach Dee Rowe soon started calling the Magic Carpet Ride. The NIT committee rewarded UConn with a second-round home game against Louisiana Tech at the Hartford Civic Center. Both Dickenman and Pikiell talked about the performance of Randy White for the visitors, who scored 23 points on 9 of 10 shooting with 10 rebounds but was scoreless in the last fourteen minutes. White was later an NBA first-round pick. UConn shot a season-high 67.5 percent from the floor in a 65–59 win.

By now, the passions were high and hopes were plentiful. Pikiell remembered how Calhoun used a numbers game to motivate the team. With the NCAA having sixty-four teams and the NIT at thirty-two, the team was told at the start that only ninety-six teams nationally were still putting on their uniforms. As UConn's wins continued and the number of teams in the combined tournaments diminished, the smaller and smaller number of those still playing was stressed to the players.

On Friday night, March 25, Calhoun's number of remaining teams had been reduced to twenty, with twelve left in the NCAA and UConn one of eight remaining in the NIT. But the matter at hand was that the Huskies were one win away from a trip to Madison Square Garden and the NIT's Final Four.

UConn was again placed at home, but this time it was at the old Field House and the opponent was Virginia Commonwealth, which entered the game with a 23–10 record. "My first memory of that night was how hot it was," said Dickenman. But most people remember the crowd. The total of 4,801 exceeded capacity, and many recall dust floating down from the rafters due to vibrations from one of the loudest UConn home crowds ever. The game was played at the Field House because the Muppet Babies had already been booked at the Hartford Civic Center, and George Thorogood and the Delaware Destroyers were playing the Richmond Coliseum, VCU's home arena.

WTIC's Joe D'Ambrosio also recalled the heat factor. "It was at least ninety degrees inside the Field House," he said. "I can still remember Jim Calhoun taking off his jacket, and he never did that."

"We could hear the crowd from inside the locker room before even coming out," said Pikiell. "Nobody had expected us to do anything, and everyone was caught up in it all."

Even with the large crowd and all the newfound passion, UConn was trailing a talented VCU team 32–29 at the half. "I'm pretty sure there are still some cracks in the wall from that halftime talk," joked Dickenman, "or perhaps a broken pane of glass."

Pikiell does not remember any coaching anger; instead he recalls Calhoun saying, "No one is going to hand us a trip to New York, and we are twenty minutes away from what we seek."

Those twenty minutes were well-played as the Huskies broke a 51–51 tie with a game-ending 21–10 run and won 72–61. "The locker room was ecstatic after," said Pikiell, "it was a 'root canal' game and everyone contributed." Indeed, the box score showed an unusually high eight players each contributed more than ten minutes of playing time. Junior Phil Gamble led UConn with 18 points, and the late Jeff King came off the bench to score all 14 of his points in the second half on his twenty-second birthday.

On Tuesday night, March 29, UConn returned to the familiar Madison Square Garden floor for the first NIT semi-final game in school history. And warming up at the other end of the court was a team in familiar uniforms, Big East foe Boston College. The Eagles came into the game with an 18–13 record and had been 6–10 in Big East regular-season play, two games better than Connecticut. The teams had split two close regular-season games. The Huskies had won in Hartford 53–49 while losing at BC 64–56.

The Eagles were led by first-team All Big East guard Dana Barros. In Barros, BC had a player combining quickness and exceptional shooting skill, especially from three-point range. And, as UConn had feared, he was on fire in the first half. Barros scored 22 points in the opening twenty minutes including 5 for 7 from three-point range. This propelled BC to a 41–33 halftime lead.

Dickenman recalls the coaches' meeting prior to talking to the team at the half. "We had to find a player to stop Barros. It was Jim's idea to put freshman Lyman DePriest on him."

Steve Pikiell said there was a toughness about Lyman. "He was calm yet cocky at the same time. It was like he knew the time had come for him to guard Barros." And guard him he did!! With DePriest on him like a blanket, Barros was held to two points in the second half, with only two shots attempted, and none from three-point range. DePriest's defense plus 74 percent Husky second-half shooting enabled Connecticut to go on an 18–4 run midway through the second half and hold on for a 73–67 win. Cliff Robinson had a superb game with 29 points to lead the team in scoring.

DePriest left UConn in 1991 as the career record holder with 132 games played. But when Connecticut fans think of Lyman, the name Dana Barros almost always comes up. It was DePriest's twenty minutes of defensive prowess on the BC star that led the Huskies into the 1988 NIT Championship game.

There was very little time to celebrate the win over BC, as the NIT Championship game was the very next night on Wednesday, March 30. For Jim Calhoun, it was the quality of the opponent that helped make this game such a special memory.

"Beating Ohio State in the championship game was very important for one reason—because it was Ohio State. They were the last team not to get in the NCAA. They had an all–Big Ten player in Jay Burson, and they were nationally regarded as a big-time team."

Another player on that Buckeye team was already well known to UConn. His name was Perry Carter. Just the name brings out emotions in Howie Dickenman. "I must have seen Perry play forty times, mainly at Gonzaga High School in Washington, D.C., but in every summer league as well. It came down to BC, Ohio State, and us. Jim worried he would choose BC and be against us in the league. We never thought he would go as far away from home as Ohio State."

Pikiell related how much Coach Dickenman and UConn wanted Carter. "I also remember a plane flew overhead at a home football game with a sign on it for Perry to come to UConn." But despite that recruiting visit to Storrs, Carter wound up in the starting line-up for the Buckeyes against the Huskies in the NIT title game.

Calhoun had one more number to show his team before the game. There were now only six teams in the country still playing—the NCAA Final Four in the upcoming weekend plus Ohio State and UConn.

The flow of the game was quite different than the night before against BC. Instead of trailing at the half, Connecticut held a slim 27–25 lead. But early into the second half, top scorer Cliff Robinson got into foul trouble. He would play just twenty-three minutes and score only five points. Junior Phil Gamble picked up the slack, playing the game of his UConn career, scoring 25 points. Tate George added 14 points with 10 assists. Freshman Murray Williams was another key player, with 11 of his 13 points coming in the second half.

The game was decided during a three-minute span in the second half, when UConn broke a 46–46 tie with a 13–2 run, building a 59–48 lead with under five minutes remaining. The Huskies went 18 for 22 from the foul line— all in the second half.

Coming in as a late-game substitute, Pikiell was handling the ball in front of the Husky bench. "Coach Calhoun was yelling at me to pass the ball, but I get fouled first. I virtually never spoke back to him, but that time I did tell the Coach to relax—meaning I'm making them, and I did."

When the final buzzer sounded and Williams threw the ball toward the roof, there was bedlam on the floor of Madison Square Garden and something close to it in thousands of living rooms in Connecticut. There had been nothing like this before in UConn sports history.

The lasting photo image of that night is of senior Jeff King and NIT Most Valuable Player Phil Gamble seated on top of the glass backboard with the final score UCONN 72 OSU 67 visible behind them. In his book *Dare to Dream*, Calhoun told Leigh Montville, "The toll keepers on the Connecticut Turnpike applauded our bus as we passed on the way back to Storrs."

The players received watches as well as rings for their championship. UConn players from the 1950s and 1960s said the watches were one of the reasons so many wanted to play in the NIT instead of the NCAA.

Back in Storrs, UConn students awaited their heroes for a celebration at the Field House. The happiness displayed by all was not only due to the first postseason championship, but simply what a huge surprise it was. Later, a ceremony was held in Hartford, with players, coaches, and all connected with the team honored at the state capitol.

On a national scale, the NIT wasn't considered important at that time, but it certainly meant everything in Connecticut. For years afterward, Calhoun would marvel at the fact that no UConn fans offered him congratulations on

Jeff King (left) and Phil Gamble on top of the backboard—and the score behind them tells why. (University of Connecticut Archives)

The Huskies celebrate the NIT Championship in Hartford. (University of Connecticut Archives)

winning the NIT. "All they said was 'thank you!'" It gave him a sense of the depth of feeling about the program. They felt it was their program and their championship as much as it was his.

And few programs have used the NIT as a springboard to success the way UConn did. Starting two years later, the Huskies would become regulars at the top of NCAA seedings on Selection Sunday. As a result, the subsequent postseason success, while thrilling, was never quite the stunner the NIT Championship was.

Perhaps it was somewhat due to Howie Dickenman picking up on the phrase, "Encourage your hopes, not your fears," as that was exactly what the Huskies did over five games between March 17 and 30 in 1988.

And then there is Tate George driving the lane making that tough bank shot in the closing seconds in the first NIT game at West Virginia. That one shot turned the tide and enabled Husky basketball to evolve into the program it is today.

The 1990 Dream Season

*Just one second left. Burrell takes the ball, looking to inbound, loops it far up court for George who catches it, turns around, shoots . . . and . . . **he got it . . . he hit it . . . He hit the shot and the Huskies have won it. . . . The Huskies have won it. . . .** George hit the shot from the right side of the lane . . . and UConn wins it 71 to 70.*

—Connecticut Radio Network play-by-play announcer
Bob Heussler's call of "The Shot" by Tate George
sending UConn into the 1990 NCAA East Regional
Final in the Meadowlands Arena.

The term "Dream Season" did not become well known in the Connecticut basketball vernacular until it was all over, but fifteen years and two national championships later, the term still brings back chills of two buzzer-beating NCAA Tournament shots — one being the most memorable shot *for* the Huskies, the other, only 43 hours later, the most painful one in UConn basketball history.

Connecticut head coach Jim Calhoun believes the transition to national prominence was in three steps, all before that 1990 NCAA Tournament. "Number one was Tate George's first-round 1988 NIT shot that led us to that championship. Number two was recruiting Chris Smith. And number three was winning our first Big East Championship," said Calhoun.

"I was heavily recruited," said Smith, a standout player at Kolbe Cathedral High School in Bridgeport, Connecticut. "North Carolina wanted me, so did N.C. State, as well as Boston College, Syracuse, and others. But Jim Calhoun said I was UConn's number one choice. He told me by coming to Storrs, I could turn the program around, and it would be a great opportunity for me. And I felt why not help my own state."

Before Smith came to Storrs, there was a long-held view that the Huskies lost out on recruiting many of the state's top high school stars. Smith mentioned John Bagley who went to BC, and Wes Matthews who played at Wisconsin, but the roots go all the way back to Hall of Famer Calvin Murphy, who in 1966 went from Norwalk High School to Niagara University. When Smith said yes to Calhoun in early 1988, even before the NIT Championship, the in-state recruiting tide had turned for UConn. And that was reinforced again a year later with the successful recruitment of Hamden's Scott Burrell.

Smith showed his talent as a freshman, but the team was somewhat disappointing. Stars Cliff Robinson and Phil Gamble were back from the 1988 NIT Championship team, yet in 1988–89, the Huskies could only finish seventh in the very strong Big East with a 6–10 league record. They lost their opening Big East Tournament game to Seton Hall, which later made it to overtime before losing the NCAA Championship game. UConn's record of 16–12 did not earn an NCAA bid, as was so eagerly anticipated in the preseason. The Huskies then failed to defend their NIT crown, losing in the third round at the Field House to Alabama–Birmingham. The final record was 18–13.

With Robinson and Gamble gone, the outlook for the following season was not promising. But there was a new determination among the returning players. "Tate George and I were named cocaptains," said Steve Pikiell. "We really worked extra hard in the spring of 1989, with the guys practicing three times a week or more at the intramural Guyer Gym."

But those practices did not include two players who were to become keys only months later. "I remember having a meal with Scott Burrell at Friendly's in Hamden," said Pikiell. "He had a lot of choices, including playing baseball, but I told him all UConn had to offer." Burrell became a first-round draft pick by baseball's Seattle Mariners but chose UConn instead. He is the only player to be a first-round pick in two sports. In 1993 he was a first-round selection of the NBA's Charlotte Hornets, and he would eventually wear a Chicago Bulls NBA Championship ring.

It was not until October that a quiet, unassuming overseas player walked into the UConn weight room. "It was all very casual," said Pikiell of the first time he saw Nadav Henefeld, a 6'7" forward from Ramat-Hasharon, Israel. No one then had any idea what Henefeld would mean to the Huskies and the state of Connecticut a few months later.

Team Bonding and Early Season Signals

The low expectations of others were firmly in place by the start of the season. Pikiell and assistant coach Howie Dickenman recalled the Huskies were expected to finish near the bottom of the league. In the preseason Big East coaches' poll, UConn was picked to be eighth in a nine-team league. But Calhoun used that to kick-start his team. "Jim was a very good motivator," said Dickenman. "He would use the Rodney Dangerfield line about lack of respect and how we were going to surprise people."

Dickenman also recalled how the season started on a positive note. "When teams take long trips, it can really help. We went to Alaska and lost our first game, but we won the next two and came back a lot closer team." Some of that promise was shown in the first Big East/ACC Challenge game against Maryland on December 4 in Hartford. UConn jumped out to a 16-point halftime lead and coasted to an 87–65 win, with Smith topping all Husky scorers with 22 points.

Yet winning in the Big East remained elusive. The Huskies were already 7–1 before their league opener in Hartford against Villanova. But when the Wildcats jumped to a 31–16 halftime lead, the team heard some boos from the home crowd. Calhoun used halftime to tell his team it was just them against the world, but a second-half rally fell short in a 64–57 loss.

It got worse at St. John's on January 2, 1990. The Redmen, as they were known then, had beaten UConn in

18 of the last 19 games going back to 1981. They again hammered the Huskies 93–62 at Alumni Hall. Dickenman recalled a postgame story. "The team was pulled off the bus by Jim Calhoun," said Dickenman. "We had left the locker room a mess with tape on the floor and ice packs all over. Jim made everyone go back in and clean it all up. Ever since, UConn has always left a locker room in better shape than they found it."

Dave Leitao, who played for Jim Calhoun at Northeastern and served for fourteen years as a UConn assistant, described an important coaches' meeting after the St. John's loss. "We were 0–2 in the league. We were discussing whether to stay with the 2-2-1 press that St. John's had shredded, and we talked about pressure defense, for and against. Jim listened to the arguments and then said we would commit to it and just do it better."

The Best January in UConn History Leads to a Title

In an odd way, that unpleasant night in Queens turned the season around. The next game on January 6 was the first Big East win of the season, a 79–61 romp over Pittsburgh in Hartford. That game was the 1,000th win in UConn history, but no one could anticipate what would soon follow.

The following week produced two road wins. The first was especially sweet, beating Villanova 71–54. Villanova was a team, like St. John's, that had dominated UConn since 1981, at one point winning fourteen straight over the Huskies. The victory avenged the Hartford loss to the Wild-

The Dream Season's "steal curtain" defense swarms archrival Syracuse. (University of Connecticut Division of Athletics)

cats less than a month before. Leitao said this road win showed the benefits of using Nadav Henefeld. "We pressed up and down court and saw how well it worked," he said.

Next, the Huskies went to Seton Hall and won 79–76. After the game Seton Hall coach P. J. Carlesimo said about Connecticut, "Quietly, they are 13 and 3, and they've played a lot of good people."

Since the formation of the Big East, the two league powerhouses consistently were Syracuse and Georgetown, each annually loaded with NBA-bound talent. The schedule had them visiting the Hartford Civic Center for back-to-back mid-January games.

The first encounter was on January 15 when UConn hosted fifth-ranked Syracuse on ESPN's *Big Monday* national telecast. The Orangemen were led by Derrick Coleman, Billy Owens, and Stevie Thompson. Unlike Carlesimo's comment, there was nothing quiet in the Hartford Civic Center when a roaring crowd saw UConn upset the Orangemen 70–59, led by 17 points each from George and Smith. The booing by Hartford fans during the Villanova game five weeks earlier was quickly forgotten.

Five nights later the other dominant Big East team, Georgetown, visited the Civic Center. If the second-ranked Hoyas won, it was expected they would be voted number one in the national polls. Georgetown was the only remaining undefeated team in the nation. "They were the original 'Evil Empire,'" quipped Pikiell. The common cliche at the time was "Hoya Paranoia." It peaked in 1990 with renowned coach John Thompson and his twin towers of 6'10" Alonzo Mourning and 7'2" Dikembe Mutombo.

By this time two elements had contributed greatly to UConn's improvement since the beginning of the season. One was the 2-2-1 press, which had been discussed after the St. John's loss and worked so well at Villanova. "We called it 'sooner or later,' meaning our press would get you at either the start or finish," said Dickenman. As many games would eventually show, "sooner or later" would be a theme throughout the year. The second key element was the increasing contributions of first-year player Henefeld and how well his skills mixed with his teammates, creating better overall chemistry.

Pikiell told a story illustrating what Henefeld brought to the team. "It was that Georgetown game, and Nadav was at the foul line very late in the game. Alonzo Mourning was a rough trash-talker, and he really was verbally abusive to the Israeli Henefeld, who calmly sank the key free throws. After the game Nadav was asked if the words upset him, and he replied that he was in the Israeli army and did duty in the Gaza Strip, so comments made in a basketball game were nothing to him."

Guard John Gwynn was a key sixth man for the Huskies. He said Henefeld "made that team better because he was extremely intelligent. He was the slowest person on our team, but he led the nation in steals. He knew how to make the players he played with better. When we lost him, it was a devastating blow." Henefeld had to return to Israel after the school year ended.

As for the "sooner or later" press, it was sooner against the Hoyas that night. Georgetown coach Thompson always wanted the other team to call the game's first time-out, but that night he was forced to call two of them in the opening minutes as Georgetown could not get the ball over midcourt against the Husky press. UConn scored the game's first 14 points, delighting the Civic Center crowd. Still, the extremely talented Hoyas tied it at 60 apiece with under four minutes to play before a three-pointer by Hene-feld and seven consecutive foul shots sealed the 70–65 win. After the game Calhoun told the media, "This is the biggest win since I have been at Connecticut." Sportscaster Joe D'Ambrosio ranks it as perhaps the most important regular-season win ever for the Huskies. Gwynn said, "After the Syracuse and Georgetown games, we knew that we were for real."

In the wake of those two signature wins came a historic week for UConn basketball. The Huskies played the final game at the Field House on January 24, beating Central Connecticut 99–79. The Field House had been UConn's home for thirty-six seasons.

On January 27 UConn opened its new on-campus home court, the Harry A. Gampel Pavilion, with a rematch against nemesis St. John's. After an embarrassing 31-point loss just twenty-five days earlier, a frenzied crowd, heavily packed with UConn students, enabled the Huskies to pull away at the end for a 72–58 win. Sophomore Dan Cyrulik played one of the best games in his UConn career, with 13 points and 10 rebounds.

Connecticut won its next three games, making it ten straight and a number eight national ranking before falling to Syracuse 90–86 at the Carrier Dome on February 10.

The Huskies rebounded with four more Big East wins before losing the rematch at Georgetown 84–64. But even with that loss, a win in the final league game at Boston College would assure UConn a piece of the Big East regular-season title.

"Jim Calhoun always had a hang-up with BC, going back to his Northeastern days," said Dickenman. "He always felt BC got too much publicity, and he took a delight in going up to Boston and beating them."

And beat them he did. Starting with the March 1988 NIT semifinal win over Boston College and ending in January 2001, Calhoun's UConn teams defeated Boston College an astounding twenty-three consecutive times, during an era when BC was usually highly competitive. But perhaps none meant more to the Husky coach than Saturday night March 3, 1990, on the BC campus.

Pikiell has a special memory of that game. "Coach Calhoun put huge emphasis on being regular-season champs, saying it meant more than the league tournament, and we felt a lot of pressure. Our sneakers were laced really tight that night. The final score (95–74) was deceiving—it was one of those 'root canal' games. The coach was really, really happy after that game. He stayed up in Boston with his family and friends but told us to go out and celebrate for what we had achieved." Indeed, that win, giving Connecticut a share of the Big East title (Syracuse beat Georgetown at home the next day to claim the other half), was the third of Calhoun's three steps that he felt made the Huskies into a national power.

Celebrating on the Garden Floor

CBS Sports, which carried the full NCAA Tournament starting in 1990, made games in the Big East Tournament at Madison Square Garden its showcase weekend telecasts leading into the NCAA selection show.

As regular-season cochampions with Syracuse, the Huskies were the number two seed in the nine-team conference field. Aside from winning the eight versus nine play-in game in 1988, UConn had not won a Big East Tournament game since 1980. Being the two seed in the tiebreaker was a disadvantage since UConn would play Friday night and, if victorious, would likely have to beat both Georgetown and Syracuse on back-to-back weekend afternoons.

But that's exactly what happened. After a relatively easy 76–58 win over Seton Hall, UConn faced powerful Georgetown for the third time that season before a Madison Square Garden sellout crowd. "Their size advantage almost was unfair," said Pikiell, "I can still remember watching Lyman DePriest trying to guard Dikembe Mutombo, who was nearly a foot taller." UConn lost starting center Rod Sellers to a knee injury after only two minutes.

The Hoyas led at the half by six. With just over thirteen minutes to go, they had a 47–39 edge, but "sooner or later" came later in this game. UConn held Georgetown scoreless for over eight minutes and ran off 14 straight points to take a 53–47 lead with under five minutes to play. Georgetown cut the lead to one, but clutch foul shooting resulted in a 65–60 Husky win, setting up the championship game showdown with Syracuse.

Sunday, March 11, 1990 was one of the great days—and early evenings—in UConn hoops history. On nationwide CBS TV, the eighth-ranked Huskies took on fourth-ranked Syracuse for the Big East Championship. The regular season cochamps would decide, on the floor of Madison Square Garden, which was the better team.

On paper Syracuse already had an edge in talent. This was accentuated by Sellers' knee injury, which limited him to two minutes in the Syracuse game. Yet, the Huskies and Orangemen were tied at 60 with fewer than eight minutes to go. "I remember saying we had played two games plus thirty-two minutes in less than three days, and the next eight minutes would tell us what we were made of," said Leitao.

They were made of pretty good stuff. With just under four minutes left, UConn took the lead for good at 67–65. Once again, key foul shooting sealed the 78–75 win. George led the Huskies in scoring with 22, including 8 for 8 from the line. Smith had 20 and was named tourney Most Valuable Player. But Gwynn scored 16 critical points in only twelve minutes, shooting 6 of 7 from the floor. And freshman forward Toraino Walker was marvelous in Sellers' absence, adding 11 points and 6 rebounds. "That was his coming-out party," said Gwynn.

As thousands of Husky fans rejoiced on the floor of Madison Square Garden, the NCAA Tournament selection committee made its final choices—and another treat was in store for all of Connecticut.

Ten Days in March—the 1990 NCAA Tournament

Perhaps the best televised sports event not involving an actual game is the *Selection Sunday* show on CBS, announcing the qualifiers and pairings for the NCAA Tournament. Pikiell remembered the team staying together in New York to watch for their seeding and location.

It could not have worked out better for the Huskies and their snowballing fan base. Not only were they rewarded with a number one seed in the East Regional, they were assigned to the Hartford Civic Center for the opening-round games. The venue choice was controversial, but since UConn had played fewer home games in Hartford than on campus, the Civic Center was technically not considered a home court by the NCAA. But, as all those who were there well recall, it certainly *sounded* like a home court!

By now all of Connecticut was in a frenzy. Nationally known *Boston Globe* sports columnist and hoops guru Bob Ryan wrote that the whole state of Connecticut had gone nuts over their amazing Huskies. Pikiell recalled the feeling: "This was much more than the NIT year. I knew we were something special when a limo took Tate and me as cocaptains plus Coach Calhoun and associate director of athletics Tim Tolokan back to Storrs from New York. Before the Hartford games, we stayed in Farmington, and loads of people wanted autographs. Everyone was coming out of the woodwork for us."

Leitao said, "There was a buzz all over the state about us. We had obtained instant credibility. I remember we were given new blue Nike warm-ups. We practiced at Central Connecticut and each one had a hundred or so fans—it was a whole different feel."

Dickenman remembered the scene awaiting the team before its first-round game in Hartford. "We could not get out of the bus to go in the Civic Center. It was a mob scene, and we had to get in through a side entrance." One reason for the huge crowd was a UConn parade at this "neutral" site!

As a top seed, the Huskies were paired against number sixteen seed Boston University, and some history fueled the pregame buildup. BU was coached by Mike Jarvis. In December 1986, during Calhoun's first season at Connecticut, the Huskies went to Boston to play the Jarvis-coached

Terriers. A near-fatal collision involving the team bus on the Massachusetts Turnpike forced the Huskies to arrive two hours late. UConn hoped for either a postponement or at least time to regroup. Instead they were told the game would begin in thirty minutes, and UConn lost 80–71, leaving hard feelings. The Huskies even lost two points at halftime because a BU student scorekeeper had missed a Cliff Robinson basket.

Jim Calhoun in the NCAA Tournament at UConn

WFAN's Mike Francesa calls Jim Calhoun a "great tournament coach"—perhaps the highest type of praise. Calhoun's record at UConn in the NCAA is especially impressive when viewed round-by-round, as follows (totals through 2004):

Round One—12 and 0
Round Two—10 and 2
Sweet Sixteen, regional semifinal—6 and 4
Regional Finals—2 and 4
Final Four, national semifinal—2 and 0
Final Four, championship game—2 and 0
TOTAL—34 wins and 10 losses in NCAA at UConn

Calhoun has been quoted as saying the hardest rounds are the first (where he is perfect at UConn), and the regional finals, the only round where he has lost more than he has won. In regional finals, UConn has had to face eventual champions UCLA and Maryland, plus national powerhouses Duke and North Carolina, with UCLA and UNC playing in their home states.

In their first NCAA game in eleven years and playing in front of virtually a home crowd, the Huskies struggled against BU for a half, leading at the break 29–28. But in the second half "sooner or later" kicked in, and an 18–1 run broke the game open, leading to a 76–52 win.

By now Connecticut's 2-2-1 press was nationally recognized. Led by Henefeld—"The Gaza Stripper"—UConn became famous for its "steal curtain" defense. Henefeld had 138 steals that year, while the Husky team had 484—both easily still stand as UConn single-season records, and the team total fell just short of the NCAA record at that time. Gwynn said the press "was effective because we had quick, athletic guys who knew how to trap."

Even legendary UCLA coach John Wooden, whose zone presses won two NCAA titles in the mid-1960s with no player over 6'5", commented on how much he enjoyed watching the way UConn played. Yet the Huskies' second-round opponent California didn't seem as impressed. Leitao remembered Cal coach Lou Campanelli saying it was no better than what they saw from Oregon in their own league.

Of course, this became immediate bulletin board material for the Huskies, and "sooner or later" was very much "sooner" in this blowout played on Saturday, March 17. After Cal's opening basket, UConn went on a 25–4 run, and the game was virtually over with eleven minutes still left in the first half. Connecticut had 16 steals and forced 28 turnovers. "We just disposed of them with our press alone," said Gwynn. "Other teams were fearful of our press." The Huskies coasted into the NCAA Sweet Sixteen with a 74–54 romp for their last game in front of the Hartford partisans.

Calhoun was in a jovial mood in the postgame when he said, "When a Campanelli coaches against a Calhoun on St. Patrick's Day, what do you expect?" Chris Smith recalled the two NCAA opponents in Hartford being "a lot easier than what we were used to in the Big East."

UConn's third appearance in the East Regionals took place at the Meadowlands Arena in East Rutherford, New Jersey. The Huskies were paired against the fifth-seeded Clemson Tigers, who won the regular-season ACC crown. The other pairing was a match of two of college basketball's icons, UCLA and Duke.

Clemson had looked lethargic at times in its two NCAA wins in Hartford, barely escaping BYU 49–47 and needing a late comeback to defeat LaSalle 79–75. But the Tigers posed the same sort of twin towers problem for the Huskies as Georgetown had earlier, with the "duo of doom"—6'11" big men Elden Campbell and Dale Davis, both of whom would go on to have long NBA careers. Still, the game seemed well in control as UConn's relentless press forced 16 first-half turnovers. With 12:36 left in the game, Connecticut led 59–40.

What followed was a "gradual eroding," as Dickenman remembered. Leitao said the early part of the game had come too easily for UConn. Smith said, "We had a five-minute stretch or so where we couldn't score and made some bad turnovers." George added, "The freshmen played like freshmen."

With only 12 seconds left, Clemson's David Young hit a corner three-pointer to give the Tigers a 70–69 lead, capping a 13–2 run. When George's 16-footer went 15 feet with less than two seconds left, the Huskies were forced to foul. Clemson's Sean Tyson missed the first of a one-and-one. By the time the Huskies rebounded and were able to call time-out, there was exactly one second remaining, and they would have to inbound from the opposite end of the court.

When celebrating its twenty-five years on the air in 2004, ESPN showed the best twenty-five sports finishes going back to 1979. Only three were chosen from college basketball, and one of them took place in that last second.

Smith, Pikiell, and Dickenman all recalled a calm huddle during the time-out. Leitao said there were some deflated faces, but Calhoun raised spirits by declaring "We are going to win!" The Huskies had practiced what they called a "home run play." Burrell showed why the Seattle Mariners wanted him to pitch for them. His pass of some 80 feet was right on target to cocaptain George who caught it to the right of the foul lane. "We knew we had to get the ball down deep with one second left," said Burrell. "We got it real close to the basket. Tate just got off a great shot and made it."

Clemson's obvious strategy was not to foul, so for the Husky faithful in attendance the first reaction to the Tate George shot was that, amazingly, he had a good look at the basket and was able to shoot cleanly. Still no one expected the ball to hit nothing but net as the horn was sounding. "I was shocked they let me get the shot up," said George.

Tate did not want to see his Husky career end after blowing a 19-point lead. He had wanted the ball to make up for his missed shot seconds before. "I thought it was over," said George. "That's been my shot. I'm thinking, 'It's been a great career, too bad it had to end that way.'"

"A lot of credit should be given to Tate, but more credit should be given to Scott," said Gwynn. "Scott nailed that right on [Tate's] hands from as far away as he was. Nobody else could have thrown that pass that far up court. That's why coach had Scott throwin' it. Because he knew."

His coach summed up the last shot, "It was a magnificent shot by a magnificent player."

The Tate George shot put the Huskies into the second NCAA Regional Final in school history. The opponent was the same team UConn played the first time back in 1964, the Duke Blue Devils. Third-seeded Duke had defeated seventh-seeded UCLA 90–81 right after the UConn win over Clemson. The Blue Devils were in the middle of one of the greatest NCAA Tournament runs ever. Their 1986 team lost the championship game to Louisville, then in 1988 and again in 1989, Duke returned to the Final Four. Thus, they were looking for a fourth Final Four visit in five years when they took the floor against UConn in the first regional final game to be played in the 1990 tournament.

Such high stakes were new for the Huskies, but fan support in the state was now enormous. Dickenman told of a poster with a thousand signatures presented to the team between the Clemson and Duke games and how moved the whole team was by this gesture.

All season long Connecticut had battled valiantly against much taller teams, but for most of the first half, it seemed the height disadvantage would finally take its toll. Duke's inside combination of sophomore forward Christian Laettner and especially senior center Alaa Abdelnaby exposed the Huskies' smaller size, and Duke opened an 11-point lead late in the half. However, UConn scored the

Tate George, the man who made "The Shot."
(University of Connecticut Division of Athletics)

final two baskets of the half and trailed by only 37–30 despite being soundly outplayed.

What followed was superb, even classic, basketball. UConn's quickness and pressure took hold early in the second half, and the game was nip and tuck down the stretch. Just as it seemed the Huskies might take control, freshman standout Burrell fouled out. Burrell's foul trouble limited him to only twenty-two minutes. When Duke senior guard Phil Henderson hit the last of his four three-pointers late, it seemed like a Husky defeat, but then Smith responded.

The Husky star shooting guard said, "I was very confident in my three-point shooting and Tate was always looking for me." With only nine seconds to go, George found Smith in transition beyond the arc to tie the game at 72 all, and when Abdelnaby's inbounds tip at the buzzer slowly rolled off the rim, the game was sent to overtime.

Both teams slowed the pace in overtime, and when a foul-lane violation gave UConn's Henefeld an extra converted foul shot, it looked like that Blue Devil error would send Connecticut to its first Final Four. In the final seconds Duke had possession trailing by one. A deflected ball almost wound up in the grasp of Tate George, but he could not control it before it hit the sideline. Thus the Blue Devils called time-out with 2.6 seconds remaining.

Pikiell said, "Had Scott Burrell not fouled out, Laettner never would have had a shot like he got." But the end result was a superbly called final play by Duke Hall of Fame coach Mike Krzyzewski. Laettner threw the inbounds pass from side court, took the return pass, and like Tate George the game before, his shot hit nothing but the bottom of the net as the horn went off to give Duke the 79–78 win.

"It was like a funeral in the locker room," said Pikiell. "We were all crying." Dickenman felt that the UConn team had let down the whole state.

It was just as personal for Leitao. "It all happened so quickly—none of us really talked about going to the Final Four. We had had so many times when we had to make a defensive stop, and I was sure we would. When I saw there were only those 2.6 seconds left, I looked behind the bench and saw a sign of Denver (the Final Four host city) with the snow-tops and all. I said to myself that we are really going to go, and of course, I put the cart before the horse."

After the game, Calhoun said, "I've always wanted to coach in a Final Four. But I'll tell you right now, I wouldn't trade this group of kids or the privilege of coaching them for a hundred Final Fours."

A former Husky great was also anticipating Denver. At the 1990 Final Four, Toby Kimball was asked to attend to be honored by the National Association of Basketball Coaches as an All-American from twenty-five years earlier. "If Laettner hadn't made that last shot, I would have been there waiting for UConn to come to the Final Four," said Kimball, who led the nation in rebounding in 1965, his senior year.

Jim Calhoun, who a week later would be named National Coach of the Year, said you cannot always write your own ending to scripts. But the return to Storrs prompted a different sort of tears, as thousands gathered in the new Gampel Pavilion to show their passionate love for this very special team. For days after, banners were on display all over the state thanking UConn for the thrills they had provided in a season that ended 31 and 6, easily breaking the Connecticut record for wins in a single year.

"Just after that season," Calhoun reflected, "a sports-writer told me the smart thing to do was leave UConn right there and then and go to one of the elite programs, where I would get to Final Fours and win National Championships. I told him no, that I wanted to stay here and do that at UConn."

As college basketball fans know, Jim Calhoun did just that, but no matter how many titles came later, no Husky fan of the era will ever forget 1989–90—the Dream Season.

Ray Allen and Big East Dominance

A flight delay might have made the difference in UConn recruiting what many still consider the best all-around player to ever wear Husky blue and white. "I'm on a recruiting trip to see a player named Kirk King in Baton Rouge, Louisiana," said long-time UConn assistant coach Howie Dickenman (King did play eventually at UConn). "I left Hartford and had to change planes in Nashville—this was around September of 1992. I was assured the plane would fly, but after waiting on the tarmac for three hours, I went into the cockpit to complain. We did not go, and I get stuck in Nashville."

It was a fortuitous stroke of good luck for UConn. Dickenman was not happy being stranded in Nashville, but he learned he had an option the next day. "There was a flight to Columbia, South Carolina, and we did have an interest in someone from Hillcrest High School in nearby Dalzell, so I flew there instead. He actually was not in our top three. But I walked in unannounced and managed to see this player named Ray Allen. As I was leaving, I saw Wake Forest head coach Dave Odom walk in, so I knew Ray was now being eagerly sought after."

Allen's college choices eventually came down to Kentucky, Alabama, and Connecticut. Dickenman said, "I remember he did decide to come up and visit us, and for some reason, we scrambled to get a new carpet in the locker room. He wore a canary-colored suit. In the end he saw that Alabama was a football school, and he felt there was a bit too much veneer at Kentucky."

Dave Leitao, also an assistant under Jim Calhoun at the time, recalled Ray's first year at UConn. "We would have team breakfasts at 7:30 and Ray would come wearing a tie. He did that every day as a frosh."

"We joked to him that this was not church," said teammate Donny Marshall, a junior when Ray Allen entered UConn as a freshman in 1993. "But Ray was just like that—always trying to do the right thing."

Marshall described the state of the UConn team as the 1993–94 season began. "The prior year Scott Burrell had been our team leader as a senior with most of us as sophomores. We missed his leadership a lot. One day we messed up at practice and Coach Calhoun was really upset with us. He was upset enough to punt some basketballs our way as we were lined up. I understood him and helped some of the other guys deal with his intensity, so I became the team leader, more or less, after Scott."

1993–94: The Huskies Begin to Exert Their Will

Jim Calhoun said, "The best team talent-wise was that '93–'94 team."

Ray Allen (left) with Coach Calhoun. (University of Connecticut Division of Athletics)

The team Ray Allen joined was poised to exceed all expectations. That was made abundantly clear in the season's second game at twelfth-ranked Virginia on November 29. The Huskies embarrassed their ACC opponents 77–36, so badly that coach Jeff Jones took out a newspaper advertisement to apologize to his team's fans for the worst home loss in Virginia history.

"We were a team full of talent," said Leitao. "The juniors were all a lot better than the year before, and Ray joined the mix smoothly." Another addition was twenty-one-year-old point guard Doron Sheffer from Ramat Efal, Israel, who immediately showed maturity.

But the star player was junior forward Donyell Marshall—not to be confused with Donny—who in his third and final UConn season put together arguably the best single season in Husky history. He averaged over 25 points per game, both overall and within the rugged Big East, while being the leading rebounder at just under 9 per game. He shot 51.2 percent for the year and simply dominated many key games. He became UConn's first consensus first-team All-American.

The team simply overwhelmed most opponents, going 15–0 at home, winning the Big East regular season with a 16–2 record, and having the nation's second-highest scoring margin over opponents at 16.3 more points per game. On March 7, UConn was ranked second nationally—the highest in school history at that point.

Donny Marshall looked back in amusement at, for him, the most memorable game of the year at Providence. "We were up by three very late, and they hit a three-pointer.

UConn's Best Regular-Season Win???

It's extremely rare for a regular-season college basketball game to become an ESPN Classic, but this one did. It was nine degrees outside with 18 inches of snow falling in Boston. It was an ESPN game with a 9:00 P.M. start on February 9, 1994, at the Conte Forum on the campus of Boston College. At that time UConn had won twelve straight over BC, dating back to 1988. The prior year Connecticut had won on the same floor thanks to a buzzer beater by Donyell Marshall. His teammate Donny Marshall discussed the passion of that midseason blizzard night: "It was the last chance against us for their veterans Billy Curley, Howard Eisley, and Malcolm Huckaby. They really hated us, as did their fans."

And BC's determination showed, as early in the second half their lead extended to 51–33. But the talented Huskies chipped away and pulled even with approximately five minutes to go. The next fifteen minutes of playing time, including both overtimes, were as hard fought as college basketball gets. With the game tied BC held the ball for a final shot in regulation but missed, and a last-second breakaway by Donyell at the buzzer failed, thus sending the game to overtime. Again in the first overtime it was tied in the closing seconds, and BC held the ball for a final shot but was once again stopped. UConn finally took the lead late in the second overtime but when Donyell Marshall could hit only one of two foul shots with just seconds to go making it 94–91, BC's one last chance to tie and force a third overtime failed. In a high-scoring game, the Husky defense prevailed. It was near midnight with the snow piling up outside before UConn fans could rejoice in a heart-pounding win in ultra-hostile territory.

Then a foul is called our way, and I get slapped with a technical for showing 'excessive emotion'; we then go down one but Kevin Ollie drives the length of the court to lay it in with seconds to go for a one-point win to save my hide. Boy did I ever give him a hug."

Both Marshalls, Ollie, Brian Fair, Rudy Johnson, and Nantambu "Boo" Willingham were part of a superb recruiting class. The group was a pleasant by-product of the 1990 Dream Season, when the nation often saw on television the up-tempo, pressure-style basketball that Jim Calhoun made his trademark.

By the postseason, hopes were high for the first visit to the Final Four. But UConn was upset by Providence 69–67 in the Big East Tournament, likely costing the Huskies a number one seed in the NCAA Tournament. Instead they were a two seed in the East behind perennial power North Carolina.

The Huskies struggled early in both their opening NCAA games against Rider and George Washington, but late-game dominance resulted in 64–46 and 75–63 wins respectively. More good news came when Boston College upset the top-seeded Tar Heels 75–72.

The Eastern Regionals were held in Miami, and as the highest remaining seed, the Huskies were favored to make it to Charlotte, site of the Final Four. The opponent was Florida, and the game followed Boston College's win over Indiana. "Our game was a late start, close to 11:00 P.M., and I think that affected our rhythm and flow," said Leitao. "Another thing was it was in Miami, one of several times we were stuck playing in the opponent's home state. And we just did not play great."

Donny Marshall still has clear memories. "They had some good players like Andrew DeClercq and Demitrius Hill. Just before the half, DeClercq stepped on my foot the wrong way. I felt some pain but kept playing. Then in the second half I saw Travis Knight was able to run past me, so I knew my foot was hurt more than I had thought." It turned out there was a fracture, which almost certainly would have kept Donny out of the regional final against BC. Marshall noted how the Huskies were eager to play BC, since UConn's winning streak against the Eagles had reached thirteen straight by the 1994 NCAA Tournament.

But UConn would not face Boston College in the regional final. A ten-point Husky lead over Florida with 14:24 remaining turned into a three-point deficit with just over five minutes to go. But victory was still within reach in a tie game when Donyell Marshall had two foul shots with three seconds to go. Yet Donyell, who had earlier gone 20 for 20 from the foul line against St. John's in Madison Square Garden, missed both shots, one twirling around the rim. The ensuing overtime was all Florida, and the highly disappointed Huskies were sent home early. Long-time WTIC play-by-play announcer Joe D'Ambrosio thought this loss was the toughest NCAA defeat ever for UConn.

Almost unnoticed in the box score was that freshman Ray Allen scored only two points in twenty minutes of playing time against Florida, a lack of production that would never occur again with him in a UConn uniform.

Three months later junior Donyell Marshall declared for the NBA draft. It was the first time a UConn player had gone to the pros early, and it made way for Allen's star to truly shine.

1994-95: Making Number One in the Polls and Noise in the NCAA

Jim Calhoun said, "The best NCAA Tournament run of any of my teams of that era."

The loss of Donyell Marshall left just one D. Marshall on the team, and he recalled low preseason expectations. "We were not ranked in the preseason top twenty-five," he said. UConn was picked third in the preseason Big East poll. "Ray really came into his own, but he had also learned about team play. He could have scored 28 or 29 a game, but he learned from Coach Calhoun."

The season's second game was UConn's first win over Duke 90–86 at the first Great Eight Tournament. Allen scored 26 points, with Ollie adding a career high 24. While the Blue Devils would eventually have a rare down season, the win was a big stepping-stone.

To the surprise of many, the team won its first fifteen games. Included in that run was a Big East game at Pittsburgh. UConn played without Donny Marshall, who was suspended for one game after an altercation in the prior contest with St. John's. The Huskies fell behind Pitt by 25 points in the first half before rallying for a stunning 85–76 win behind Allen's 27 points and 8 rebounds. D'Ambrosio recalls that game vividly. "First for our broadcast, it was a miserable trip and the Fitzgerald Field House was a tough place to play. Then we trail by 40–15, but I remember our broadcast location was right next to the UConn bench and that night Jim Calhoun was very positive throughout."

Syracuse made its only visit to Gampel Pavilion that season on ESPN's *Big Monday* and led 58–47 with fewer than twelve minutes remaining. But three-pointers by Sheffer and Ollie capped the UConn comeback in an 86–75 win. ESPN's Dick Vitale called Storrs The Basketball Capital of the World.

The next game was in Kansas City, a nationally televised game against Kansas. However, the Huskies shot just 26 percent and were clobbered by one of the nation's elite programs, 88–59.

Yet that defeat was shaken off, and after three more Big East wins, the Huskies traveled to Syracuse on Sunday, February 12. With an 18–1 record, a win at the Carrier Dome was expected make UConn the nation's number one team. The 77–70 victory put the Huskies atop both polls the next day. UConn's first game at number one was a 91–85 win at Georgetown, as the Huskies converted 27 of 32 free throws, including nine straight in the final minute.

The lofty status lasted just six days. The following Saturday Villanova came into Gampel Pavilion, where UConn was usually invincible, and routed Connecticut 96–73. And some three weeks later Villanova hammered the Huskies again 94–79 in the Big East Championship Game. "I played pro ball with Kerry Kittles," said Donny Marshall, "and I told him how many times we had to do Coach's suicide drills (running and touching foul lines) due to how his teams handled us."

Allen scored his 1,000th career point in the Big East title game, joining Wes Bialosuknia as the first two players in Connecticut basketball history to accomplish that feat in just two years of playing.

Three of UConn's four losses had been by big margins, but the team had gone 16–2 to once again be regular-season

Big East Champions, this time by a league record three-game margin. The Huskies felt good as the number two seed in the NCAA West Regional. Federal Way, Washington, native Donny Marshall anticipated a trip to the Final Four in nearby Seattle.

Unlike some years when UConn had struggled in opening-round games, the Huskies scored the game's first 15 points and routed an overmatched Tennessee–Chattanooga team 100–71 in Salt Lake City. The second game against seventh-seed Cincinnati was much tougher, but clutch foul shooting late in the game helped the Huskies prevail, 96–91. UConn shot 67 percent in the second half and set a school record by making fifteen three-point hoops.

The West Regionals were in Oakland, and the Sweet Sixteen matchup was against third-seeded Maryland. "We were actually scared of them from all we had heard, especially that Joe Smith was the best player in college basketball," said Donny Marshall, "but Coach Calhoun won that game for us with superb strategy." UConn attacked Smith and got him in early foul trouble. The game was an example of scoring runs, quick spurts that were UConn's high-octane trademark. They usually resulted in wins, breaking open an otherwise tight game. Against Maryland it was a 21–6 run early in the second half for a 70–51 lead in a 99–89 win. Smith was held to 10 points in the first twenty-eight minutes.

Standing in the way of the Final Four was the best team in the country—this time wearing the storied letters U-C-L-A across their jerseys. And as had been true with Florida in Miami the prior year, and three years later with North Carolina in Greensboro, UConn would have to get to the Final Four by winning in the home state of its opponent.

UCLA became the 1995 national champion, but the Bruins had a huge scare in the second round. Against Missouri they were saved by a court-length drive by star guard Tyus Edney, whose lay-up at the buzzer gave UCLA a 75–74 win. But by the time they took the floor against UConn for the West Regional Final, the fabled Bruins looked like a vintage John Wooden team of twenty-five or so years earlier.

Marshall felt it was close enough to taste. It was his dream to go to his home area of Seattle for UConn's first Final Four appearance, but it was not to be. "It was their freshmen, Toby Bailey and J. R. Henderson, that did us in," he said. The Huskies kept it close most of the way but lost 102–96. However, that defeat by UCLA showed more than ever what an emerging superstar the Huskies had in Ray Allen. The silky smooth sophomore poured in 36 points, a then UConn record for an NCAA game. (It was matched nine years later by Ben Gordon against Alabama.) Famed former coach Al McGuire, doing the TV color commentary, raved about Ray, saying if he stayed through his senior year he would be the best player in America. UCLA coach Jim Harrick said, "Ray Allen is the best player we've faced this season."

Calhoun remains especially wistful about this team. "If Edney does not make that end-to-end play against Missouri to win for UCLA, we would have not only gone to the Final Four, but we would have easily defeated Oklahoma State in the national semifinals. This team gave me the best fast-break basketball I had, until our 2004 NCAA games."

1995–96: Record Winning Streak and League Supremacy

Jim Calhoun said, "The best team play, as in T-E-A-M, that I ever had."

With leaders such as Donny Marshall and Kevin Ollie gone, the transition was made to another team that holds a special place in the heart of Jim Calhoun. He quickly spins out the players: "We had Kirk King, Rudy Johnson, Travis Knight, Ray Allen, and Doron Sheffer, as starters with Ricky Moore, Eric Hayward, and Rashamel Jones off the bench — that was it, an eight-man team."

While Allen was the superstar, the floor leader for all three seasons was Sheffer. He was a poised playmaker who also scored in double figures each year.

The season began at the Great Alaska Shootout with a win over TCU. The next game was indeed a "shootout," with an overtime loss to Iowa 101–95, but this was followed by a rout of Indiana 86–52, one of the worst losses ever suffered by a Bobby Knight team. It was November 25, and no one could then imagine it would be close to three months before the Huskies would taste defeat again.

There was a scare on December 3 when Boston College came within a point, but UConn's 63–62 win extended a near eight-year streak over the Eagles to 16 games. By January 21, Connecticut had won 14 straight and was ranked fifth in the nation when number twelve-ranked Syracuse came to Hartford for a national TV game. Their star John Wallace was talented and a talker. Well into the second half, Wallace verbally challenged Allen. The Husky star responded with actions not words and took over the game for a 79–70 win. Allen finished with 27 points.

By now it was clear that there were three dominant teams in the country, with UConn one of them. The other two were Kentucky, restored to glory by coach Rick Pitino, and Massachusetts, led by star center Marcus Camby of Hartford, a player Connecticut had coveted. The media, from Vitale on down, loudly lamented the two long-time Yankee Conference foes did not schedule each other, but they had not played since early 1990.

The Huskies' focus was on their own league, not the next-door rivals from the past, and the streak ended at a school-record twenty-three wins when the Huskies hit the road and fell to eleventh-ranked Georgetown and All-American Allen Iverson, 77–65. In the enlarged conference it was the only regular-season clash of the Huskies and Hoyas, but there would be a postseason return match.

"The league was really great that year," recalled D'Ambrosio. "UConn, Georgetown, and Syracuse were all at their best." Indeed the Huskies and Hoyas wound up as number one and number two seeds respectively in the NCAA, while the fourth-seeded Orangemen made it to the NCAA Championship game.

It was a poignant senior night at Gampel on February 28 against Rutgers. Jim Calhoun warmly embraced several playing their last UConn home game including stalwarts such as Sheffer and center Travis Knight. The unspoken aspect of the night was that almost all in attendance knew it would also be the last home game for junior Ray Allen. After Rutgers shocked the Huskies jumping off to a 15-point first-half lead, Ray put on a scoring show, pouring in a career-high 39 in the 78–66 come from behind win. Allen tied a Big East record by making nine three-point field goals.

Despite regular-season league dominance, UConn had won the Big East Tournament only once—in the 1990 Dream Season. With relatively easy wins over Seton Hall and Syracuse, the championship game was with the Hoyas and future top–NBA draft pick Iverson.

"The first four minutes of that game were a great brand of basketball," said D'Ambrosio who called the game on radio. "It was a racehorse game up and down the court."

But after that, the Huskies were clearly outplayed and down 11 after Knight fouled out with 4:46 remaining. But Georgetown didn't score again. The winning bucket was an off-balance foul-line jump shot by Allen, who initially was looking to pass while airborne. "I jumped up in the air," said Allen, "and I was going throw it to Rudy, but they denied him, so I threw it up at the last second. I can't believe it went in." The awkward shot rolled in with 13 seconds left, and UConn survived three missed Georgetown buzzer beaters. Allen had missed his previous fourteen shots. Rarely big scorers, forward Kirk King and freshman guard Ricky Moore combined to score the remaining 20 of UConn's final 22 points. The Huskies scored the game's last 12 points in a thrilling 75–74 win for the Big East Tournament Championship. "One of the great athletic contests I've ever been involved in," said Calhoun.

The win over Georgetown made third-ranked UConn a number one seed in the NCAA Southeast Regional in Indianapolis. Expectations were very high for that elusive first Final Four appearance, but unlike the prior year, this UConn team did not click in the national tournament. The

Ray Allen—quite possibly the greatest all-around player in UConn basketball history. (University of Connecticut Division of Athletics)

opening game against number sixteen–seeded Colgate resulted in an early 36–17 lead but only a 9-point win and more important a severe shoulder injury to Moore. Then the Huskies had to rally from a 13-point first-half deficit to overcome Eastern Michigan 95–81. Doron Sheffer had a career-high 27.

The regionals were in Lexington, Kentucky, and UConn was paired against a dangerous foe. While only seeded fifth, Mississippi State had decisively upset Kentucky in the SEC Tournament Championship game. The Bulldogs had hot outside shooting in the first half and held UConn to a season low of 32.4 percent. The Huskies rallied from 14 down with 6:50 to go to trail by only three, but when a last minute three-pointer by Allen missed, UConn went down to defeat 60–55.

While that season had a disappointing ending, Jim Calhoun looks back at the three years of UConn with Ray Allen and Doron Sheffer with enormous pride. "We went 49 and 5 in league play and 17 and 1 in Ray's last year. The league was full of top players like Iverson, Kittles, and Billy Curley of BC. It took us seven or eight years to get to that level, but no one had dominated the league like that before, and I feel no one will again." Allen's Husky teams never spent a day out of first place in the Big East in his three seasons.

While the goal of a Final Four visit remained elusive, the record book bears out Calhoun's sense of pride and accomplishment. That airport delay which led to Howie Dickenman's unplanned visit to Dalzell, South Carolina, triggered an unforgettable three years of Husky success and thrills.

The Promised Land— The 1999 Championship

In the spring of 1998, two sets of parents contributed to what became total Husky jubilation at the end of March 1999.

North Carolina ended UConn's 1997–98 season in the NCAA East Regional Final at the Greensboro Coliseum— virtually a home game for the Tar Heels. Ushers handed out Carolina Blue pom-poms to patrons at the ostensibly "neutral" venue. Connecticut coach Jim Calhoun said that North Carolina team, which had Vince Carter, Antawn Jamison, and superb point guard Ed Cota, was the most talented team UConn has ever faced in the NCAA Tournament. After the game, the parents of UConn freshman point guard Khalid El-Amin boarded the team bus to say how proud they were of all the Huskies and how they would all be together for the Final Four the next year.

Another set of parents played a crucial role in the success of the following season. Star sophomore Richard "Rip" Hamilton was highly tempted to leave UConn after two seasons and go to the NBA, where it was felt he would be a mid-to-late first-round pick.

Assistant coach Tom Moore remembers the importance of that decision-making time. "Not only might we lose Rip, but Kevin Freeman was hearing a lot of advice to transfer from UConn to a program where he could play the wing forward position and be a star, rather than his power forward role at Connecticut. Rip and Kevin were extremely close, and we felt Kevin was waiting for Rip's choice."

Moore felt Hamilton would leave UConn. "Our offices were all close together. Rip comes to tell me he is leaving, and he tells assistant coach Dave Leitao the same thing. Then he goes into Coach Calhoun's office where his parents are, and they wanted him to stay. About thirty minutes later, Rip comes out and says all has changed—he is staying. Of course, Kevin then stayed as well."

The Husky coaching staff heaved a huge sigh of relief, and comments Calhoun made immediately after the North Carolina loss became more realistic. "Jim started talking about Tropicana Field (site of the 1999 Final Four) immediately after we lost in 1998," said Tom Moore.

Rashamel Jones, a four-year Husky contributor who played 132 career games, recalled the preseason attitude. "It was in our heart; it was burning. In '99 we were just hungry."

In modern college basketball with early departures to pro ball common, a full returning starting five was a rarity.

But the Huskies started the 1998–99 season with just that. Senior guard Ricky Moore was joined by three juniors—Hamilton, Freeman, and center Jake Voskuhl—plus sophomore floor leader El-Amin.

Coach Moore was emphatic about the importance of El-Amin. "I firmly believe he was the most important recruit ever for UConn. His personality was exactly what that team needed. He had a swagger about him." There remains an ongoing argument about who is the greatest high school basketball player in Minnesota history: the two choices are Celtic Hall of Famer Kevin McHale and El-Amin.

El-Amin's first visit to UConn, at a time when coaches were prevented from on-court time with a recruit, is legendary. "He took over a practice session with returning players he never had met before. He picked the teams, refereed as he played, even did play-by-play," laughed Tom Moore.

El-Amin is more modest about his leadership role. "I never thought about what I was doing, it was just my personality." He added, "What we had at UConn was a special bond. I've been on many teams, but at Connecticut it was more than coach-player roles. We were a tight-knit family."

El-Amin and assistant coaches Leitao and Moore all mentioned the value of the preseason trip to England and Israel. "The guys could be a bit freer and let their hair down a bit," said Leitao. "And we were later oddly helped out by the NBA lockout when past UConn stars like Ray Allen, Scott Burrell, and Travis Knight went up against the present team in practice. They played us seriously and it helped."

Virtually every preseason poll had either UConn or Duke as number one. When the Blue Devils were upset by

Cincinnati 77–75 on November 28, the door was opened for the Huskies to be a consensus number one, and they stayed in the top spot in both polls for all of December and January.

The 19–0 start included three signature wins in a twelve-day span in December. On December 1, the UConn Huskies had a rematch with the Washington Huskies in the Great Eight Tournament in Chicago. Nine months earlier, Hamilton's fall-away jumper at the buzzer gave Connecticut a 75–74 win over Washington in the NCAA East Regional Semifinals. In Chicago, El-Amin sparked a 20–2 second-half run in a 69–48 win.

Four days later, UConn defeated Final Four–bound Michigan State 82–68 at Gampel Pavilion. Ricky Moore's block of MSU All-America guard Mateen Cleaves was the showstopper. Moore held Cleaves to 2 of 15 shooting—a common denominator among guards Moore defended. "He didn't have to score," said Jones. "His job was to play defense. Ricky was our glue."

And on December 12, Freeman's steal of an inbounds pass set up El-Amin's 13-footer in the lane with 2 seconds left in a 70–69 win before an incredibly hostile crowd at Pittsburgh's Fitzgerald Field House. Pitt led by 4 points with 10 seconds left.

In a game that typified the determination of the 1999 UConn team, Ricky Moore rallied the Huskies from a 12-point deficit with seventeen minutes remaining in a physical and emotional 78–74 win over ninth-ranked St. John's at Madison Square Garden.

However, Hamilton (thigh) and Voskuhl (foot) suffered injuries in that game, forcing them both to miss the

February game two nights later against Syracuse in Hartford, a poorly played 59–42 loss. Up next was a cross-country trip to Stanford, with the Cardinal eager to avenge a 20-point loss to UConn the prior year at Gampel. Voskuhl was medically cleared to play, but the Huskies were still without top scorer Hamilton and facing a very hostile crowd.

Jones recalls the superb performance of the whole team but especially El-Amin. "There was a lot of heckling going on in that game, and he went out and showed them his game. He was on fire in the first half, and he put us on his back." The Huskies jumped to a 17–4 lead. El-Amin scored 16 points in a brilliant first half. When Stanford closed to within 2 points late, Husky foul shooting was clutch, resulting in a 70–59 win at Maples Pavilion.

Aside from a 73–71 upset loss to Miami at Gampel, Connecticut went unblemished the rest of the way, winning another Big East regular-season title. "We learned from that game," said Jones. Still, the 1998–99 Huskies were all about what would happen in the NCAA Tournament.

El-Amin felt UConn's dominating performances in the Big East Tournament over Syracuse 71–50 and St. John's 82–63 for the championship were a big help in getting the team ready for the NCAA. "We really kicked rear ends," he joked. The Most Outstanding Player of the Big East Tournament was Kevin Freeman, the often overlooked power forward, and the choice delighted his teammates and coaches. "Kevin was our enforcer down low," said Jones. "He was like our bully down low. He was a defensive animal. I used to love watching 'KFree' play defense."

The Huskies knew they would be a number one seed, just not where. Duke had not lost since that late November game and was the East's top seed as the nation's top-ranked team. While UConn had beaten powerful Michigan State in December, the Spartans had dominated all opponents after that and were ranked second nationally by the Associated Press and as the top seed in the Midwest Regional. That left third-ranked UConn to be the top seed in the West, with the opening rounds in Denver. This was a popular choice, as Big East teams had a history of doing well in the West Regional.

Unlike many prior years when the brackets contained obvious obstacles for UConn, the Huskies had what appeared to be a favorable draw. However, analysts mentioned that tenth-seed Gonzaga was a tougher team than most would think—and indeed it was!

Before the Huskies took the court for their first NCAA game, a birth and a death each affected the team. The birth was Jim Calhoun's first grandchild, and his accompanying pride may have released some of the stress of getting to his first Final Four. Emily was born on March 5, the day UConn defeated Syracuse in the Big East Tournament semifinals.

The death, from long-term illness, was former team manager Joe McGinn, which, while expected, impacted everyone in the UConn basketball family.

Assistant coach Dave Leitao told of the team practicing at the Air Force Academy in Colorado Springs when hearing the news of McGinn's passing. "We were given a quote in memory of Joe saying life is a journey of a butterfly. Then later, on each of our hotel room doors we found a small plaque of a butterfly. It was very moving."

Just prior to the game against sixteenth-seeded Texas–San Antonio, Calhoun came down with a stomach virus and could not coach. Leitao took over for the game, and while UConn started slowly, the Huskies took control late in the first half and coasted to a 91–66 win.

Up next were the Lobos of New Mexico, the early game of a second-round afternoon doubleheader. A main task of assistant coach Tom Moore was to learn all he could about the opponent and prepare the team for what they would face. El-Amin still remembers the film clips of the Lobos shown before the game. "We watch this film—nothing but their very best highlights, enough to make us fear them. I remember coming to tears at the pregame prayer over the thought this could be our last game. The guys really rallied around before that game."

Khalid's pregame fears came to naught. Like Husky fans, New Mexico supporters stand until their team scores its first point. The red-clad contingent of Lobo fanatics stood, and stood, and stood. UConn scored the game's first 17 points, forcing New Mexico fans to ache for the chance to finally sit down. Another intimidating run of 13 points at the start of the second half boosted the Husky lead to 50–22, and UConn easily advanced to the Sweet Sixteen with a 78–56 win.

The second game of the doubleheader would determine the Huskies' next opponent. It was a blazing quick Arkansas team against Iowa. The latter was coached by Dr. Tom Davis, who had already been told he would not return to coach the following year. While the speedy Razorbacks looked like they would be a very challenging potential foe for UConn, the inspired Iowa Hawkeyes played rugged, physical basketball and rallied from a 47–34 deficit to win 82–72 for their outgoing coach.

As the Iowa-Arkansas game unfolded, the other scores coming in from the regional seemed to clear the path all the more for UConn. Second-seeded Stanford was shocked by upstart Gonzaga, and third-seeded North Carolina had been sent home by Weber State in the first round. Those upsets, plus having fourth-seeded Arkansas also out, made the Huskies a prohibitive favorite in the West Regional, which took place in Phoenix.

Being the heavy favorite might sound good, but the games played out far differently. Iowa was inspired to pull off another upset for the departing coach. Calhoun said it was the most physical game that any of his teams had ever played. With only ten minutes to go, the game was tied at 53–53, but UConn outscored their Big Ten opponent by holding them to four points over the next eight minutes to lead 67–57 with just over two minutes to play. Another series of clutch foul shots clinched the 78–68 win, putting UConn in its fourth regional final of the 1990s.

In the prior three regional finals since 1990, UConn was paired against hoops icons Duke, UCLA, and North Carolina. This time it was tiny Gonzaga from Spokane, Washington, and it was hard to tell if the name of this little known college was harder to spell or pronounce. At the time Gonzaga (gone-ZAG-uh) was virtually unknown in hoops circles, as it was the 1999 tournament that started its rise to national prominence. But the Zags had defeated three big-time teams — Minnesota, Stanford, and Florida, the last in overtime — to make their first regional final. While NBA all-star John Stockton played there, the most famous alumnus of the small Jesuit college in eastern Washington State was Bing Crosby.

UConn was a heavy favorite, considering it was a regional final. While the upside of the Huskies making it to their first Final Four was obvious, the downside was also enormous. This was the sixth time in the decade UConn had been seeded first or second in an NCAA regional, and after the 1996 upset loss to Mississippi State, a New York tabloid had labeled the Huskies "UCan't" referring to Sweet Sixteen defeats.

The sold-out America West Arena in Phoenix was some 1,000 miles from the Gonzaga campus, but the largest college basketball crowd ever to see a game in Arizona adopted the underdog Zags, making it a virtual road game for Connecticut. "There was tension all over," said Joe D'Ambrosio, who did the radio play-by-play. "It was like the Kenny Loggins song 'This Is It.'"

When asked if this was the most nerve-racking game in his ten seasons as a UConn assistant, Tom Moore said, "That's one hundred percent right. Not much was said out loud, but we were petrified to lose, and that fan noise for them was loud and clear."

Leitao agreed. "That was really a hard fought game. They were quicker and tougher than expected. Their point guard Quentin Hall was as quick as we faced all season."

Rashamel Jones said the Iowa and Gonzaga games were tougher than the Final Four games that followed.

El-Amin picked up two fouls in the first four minutes guarding Hall and went to the bench for the rest of the half. But Ricky Moore filled the scoring void, and the Huskies trailed by only 32–31 at halftime. UConn shot just 37 percent for the game, by far its lowest in postseason play. Incredibly, El-Amin shot 0 for 12 from the floor.

With six minutes to go, the teams were tied at 55 each, but UConn built a 63–59 lead with a minute remaining. Then the speedy Hall threw in a long off-balance three-pointer with 36.6 seconds left to put hearts in the throats of every Husky fan. That shot made it 63–62, but the Zags would not score again. After two clutch El-Amin foul shots, Gonzaga was stopped on its next possession. Two more free throws by Freeman with 6.2 seconds remaining sealed the win, and it was Freeman who threw the ball skyward as the buzzer sounded, signifying the long wait for a Final Four trip for the Huskies was finally over.

As the first team to qualify for the 1999 Final Four, Connecticut and its fans could sit back and watch who would join them. The Huskies would face the winner of third-seeded St. John's against fourth-seeded Ohio State from the South Regional. The idea of facing tough league-foe St. John's a third time within the Final Four setting was not appealing, but the OSU Buckeyes held off a Red Storm rally to advance 77–74. The next day, the two expected top-seeded powers, Duke and Michigan State, each won their regional finals easily. That meant an unusually strong quartet, including three number one seeds, would gather for the Final Four at Tropicana Field in St. Petersburg.

It was a relaxed and humorous Jim Calhoun who spoke at the Final Four coaches' event. He gave the expected "glad to see you here" greetings to Duke's Mike Krzyzewski and Michigan State's Tom Izzo, but he then turned to the Ohio State coach who would oppose him next and said, "and I am *very* happy to see you here, Jim." The quip was based on Calhoun's amazing victory streak of 19 straight over Jim O'Brien's Boston College teams from 1988 to 1997.

Sandwiched between the heart-pounding victory over Gonzaga to get to the Final Four and the classic championship game against Duke, much less is remembered about the semifinal defeat of Ohio State. Against another rugged Big Ten opponent, the Huskies regained their shooting touch, making 47 percent for the game. While Ohio State was always within striking distance, the Huskies held the Buckeyes to just 24 percent shooting in the second half and won 64–58. Hamilton continued his torrid NCAA scoring run, leading the Huskies with 24 points.

Senior Rashamel Jones recalled a moment that pulled the team together the night before the championship game. "All our players were watching TV together in a hotel room but Coach was not there. ESPN was showing Durham, North Carolina, where they had printed up T-shirts and everything with Duke, and we're watching this, like, are you serious? We haven't even played the game yet, and they've got T-shirts and balloons made up. That's a slap in our face. You know what, tomorrow we're gonna beat Duke."

But the oddsmakers and the national media seemed to agree with the Blue Devil partisans. UConn entered the championship game with a record of 33–2 and had been ranked number one for a solid two months. However, the Huskies were still a 9½-point underdog to a Duke team that was 37–1 and had won 32 straight since their lone loss four months earlier to Cincinnati. Three months after the championship game, four of the top fourteen first-round NBA picks were from the Duke team that took the floor against the Huskies at Tropicana Field.

Still, Calhoun remained relaxed and confident. Between UConn's Final Four games, the coach spent time

Khalid El-Amin—"we shocked the world." (University of Connecticut Archives)

with his family in the hotel lobby, really enjoying little Emily.

D'Ambrosio's memory of the pregame was revealing. "The UConn players seemed unusually relaxed and casual. The Duke players seemed to come across like a group feeling they were in trouble and went out of their way to give lots of credit to Connecticut."

Before the game Tom Moore gave the Huskies and their coaches his rundown on the opponent, giving Duke's key strengths and weaknesses—far more of the former. When his assistant finished the briefing, Jim Calhoun turned to him and said, "It seems like even some assistant coaches believe Duke is invincible." To Calhoun, the Blue Devils were not that. "Yes, they had talent," said Calhoun when interviewed for this book, "but we had more experience and more toughness, and I will take that combination every time." Calhoun's confident, relaxed approach could be seen throughout his first-ever coaching experience in the Final Four.

The game that followed was voted by an ESPN fan poll as the best NCAA Championship game of the 1990s and has been written about extensively. But it did not start well for the Huskies, with Duke jumping off to a 9–2 lead. Jones said of his fellow senior, Ricky Moore, "We were definitely in trouble, and he was the catalyst." Moore, known for his defense and floor leadership, scored all 13 of his points in the first half.

Tom Moore also admitted to being worried during Duke's opening burst. Leitao recalled, "We took an early time-out and said what are we doing here, but we did a great job to settle down." Once Ricky's surprise early scoring got the Huskies back in the game, the remainder of the first half was nip and tuck. A Trajan Langdon three-pointer just before the buzzer gave Duke a 39–37 lead at the half.

In the second half the complexion changed. UConn simply looked like the better team. Rip Hamilton was on fire, and midway through the second half, CBS analyst Billy Packer declared: "He is sensing that nobody out there can guard him—and that is saying something." With fewer than eight minutes to go, the Huskies were up by six. Tom Moore remembered a time-out with Kevin Freeman in front of the Duke bench, "They were tired and Kevin heard some bickering. He returned to our bench and said 'they ain't got it' and said it loudly enough for Duke to hear, yet there was no reply from them."

Rip Hamilton shoots over Elton Brand during the Huskies' victory over Duke, arguably the greatest game in UConn history. (University of Connecticut Division of Athletics)

Top Husky Players under Jim Calhoun

Donny Marshall wanted no part of choosing a first and second team of UConn players under Jim Calhoun, as he thought there were too many good players to omit anyone. However, several contributed to choosing the list below, though the choices indeed were very tough to make. The coauthors, long-time UConn associate director of athletics Tim Tolokan, and WTIC's Joe D'Ambrosio all agreed on the following:

First Team:

Donyell Marshall (forward)
Caron Butler (forward)
Emeka Okafor (center)
Ray Allen (guard)
Rip Hamilton (guard)

Second Team:

Scott Burrell (forward)
Cliff Robinson (forward/center)
Chris Smith (guard)
Khalid El-Amin (guard)
Ben Gordon (guard)

Yet, the Blue Devils did come back. With 3:50 to play, two Hamilton foul shots gave the Huskies a 70–68 lead, and 21 seconds later Rip's "bodacious" (his word) three-pointer from left of the lane would be Connecticut's last field goal of the game. Duke cut the lead to 75–74 with under a minute to go, and when El-Amin missed on a driving layup with 24 seconds to go, the Blue Devils had the ball and their chance to win. But thanks to Ricky Moore's defense, Langdon traveled, and it was Husky ball with a time-out called and only seconds to go.

Both Tom Moore and El-Amin recall the discussion during the time-out. A successful inbounds pass was essential, and if completed, UConn wanted a top foul shooter to get it. The play Calhoun considered was called a "14," but El-Amin and Tom Moore felt another inbound play called "Diamond" would effectively get it to the floor leader and maximize the chances for two made free throws. Calhoun agreed with going to Diamond for the inbound, and as hoped, El-Amin was fouled and sent to the line.

On many Connecticut walls there is a wide-angle deluxe photo from the Rob Arra collection taken at Tropicana Field. El-Amin stands at the foul line with 5.2 seconds showing on the overhead scoreboard; he holds the ball for his second shot after having made the first. That second shot was also made and the Husky lead became 77–74, which was the final score when Langdon was again stopped.

Rashamel Jones was on the court for the final seconds. He recalled forcing the final turnover along with Ricky Moore, and he held the ball as the buzzer sounded. "It was definitely special, just to have the ball, to be a senior. This

The moment of glory—March 29, 1999. (University of Connecticut Division of Athletics)

is your final game and to be moving on. There is nothing better than that. It was a storybook ending."

Jim Calhoun led his team as they cut down the nets in UConn's finest hoops moment, but one strand was left on the rim. It was to commemorate Joe McGinn, a member of the team in spirit looking down from above at the celebrating Huskies.

As for what Jim Calhoun had achieved, former head coach Dee Rowe may have put it best in a recent comment: "Jim Calhoun has taken UConn basketball to the top of the mountain, to a place never before even dreamed of. He has truly performed a miracle."

With Final Four Most Outstanding Player Rip Hamilton headed for the NBA draft after three years at UConn, and Ricky Moore a senior, all knew the Husky starting five had ended their playing days together. Over two seasons these five starters combined to go 66 and 7 with a national championship. And yet, they would indeed appear as a unit once more.

On August 14, 2004, at the second Jim Calhoun Charity Classic game of former Husky greats, close to thirty players from his eighteen seasons as coach returned, with teams divided into blue and white jerseys for the exhibition game. When the white team took the floor, there were Ricky, Rip, Khalid, Kevin, and Jake all together again. The thoughts of the hard-core partisans attending could not help but return to the night of March 29, 1999, in St. Petersburg—the greatest night in UConn basketball history.

The Second Crown: The 2004 Huskies

P ut the covers of the November 24, 2003, and April 12, 2004, issues of *Sports Illustrated (SI)* side by side and you have the bookends of expectations and meeting them. The former shows Diana Taurasi and Emeka Okafor standing together as *SI* declared UConn preseason number one in both women's and men's basketball. The latter issue shows Emeka alone (the women's championship was played a day too late for that issue). His arms are raised high and across the center of the cover in very large type is the word DOMINANT.

And yet, as all avid UConn fans know, the 2003–04 NCAA Champion Huskies had their share of bumps and bruises, literal as to the latter, in between those two magazine issues.

It started a year earlier at the same place it would end, the Alamodome in San Antonio, where the scoreboard read TEXAS 82 CONNECTICUT 78 after the Longhorns had knocked the Huskies out of the 2003 NCAA Tournament in the Sweet Sixteen. That painful score was written down by then junior reserve forward Shamon Tooles. "I wrote it on my sneaker in the locker room," said Tooles, "to be a reminder throughout the year of how much that loss hurt. We somehow felt cheated and robbed." The Alamodome was also to be the site of the 2004 Final Four. Once Connecticut head coach Jim Calhoun congratulated his seniors, he wasted no time letting the returning players know that the goal was to return to the same floor for the Final Four next year.

Tooles was an excellent behind-the-scenes example of why UConn has had such great team play for so many years. Wearing number 30 for his full four seasons, Tooles gave a total effort off and on the court. He was described as a "tireless worker in the paint," but he played very few minutes in most games for much of his career. Husky assistant coach Tom Moore told this story about Tooles as the team prepared for 2003–04. "He comes to Coach Calhoun before the season starts and tells him not to worry about his playing time. Shamon knew we were loaded with depth up front, and he just told Coach he would keep working hard and there was no need to give him playing time just based on hard work."

Tooles confirmed the story when interviewed. "Yes, I told the Coach not to worry about my minutes. I will give the same work ethic."

Moore, Tooles, and everyone else knew how talent-laden this team was. Virtually the entire team that made it to the Sweet Sixteen the year before was returning, including two preseason All-Americans in Okafor and Ben Gordon. New additions, especially big men Josh Boone and Charlie Villanueva, made UConn one of the more imposing college teams, based on pure talent, in recent years—at least on paper.

But games are not played on paper, and the Huskies tasted their first adversity on November 26 in Madison Square Garden in the semifinals of the Preseason NIT Tournament. The opponent was Georgia Tech, which was not even picked to make the sixty-five-team NCAA Tournament field in that preseason *SI* issue. But it was the Yellow Jackets who looked like a top-flight team in a convincing 77–61 defeat of UConn. Especially worrisome was back pain, which severely limited Okafor's effectiveness. Another concern was horrendous 10 for 30 foul shooting, UConn's worst under Calhoun, and it was a weakness that would continue throughout the regular season. No one could imagine that night that the two teams would meet again more than four months later with vastly higher stakes.

The Huskies bounced back to win their next eleven games and were especially impressive in a nationally televised rout of Oklahoma at Gampel Pavilion by an 86–59 margin in a game not even that close. UConn led by 40 points early in the second half. But adversity was to strike again from mid-January to mid-February, with four losses in a nine-game stretch.

The first of these was at North Carolina on January 17. Reserve guard Justin Evanovich said, "It was our second year in a row visiting them at the Dean Dome in Chapel Hill. Both times we lose in the final seconds, and their fans storm the floor, thrilled to beat us. We were still finding ourselves, and perhaps some of the young guys were playing without a sense of urgency."

Yet even in that defeat, the potential of this team was recognized. CBSSportsline.com college basketball columnist Gregg Doyell wrote that he had just seen the best college basketball team in five seasons, since 1999, and despite the loss, it was UConn. Doyell compared these Huskies, not to the UConn NCAA Champions of that year, but to the Duke team they beat, a Blue Devils team that featured four of the first fourteen players selected in the NBA's 1999 draft.

While Doyell was convinced UConn was the best team in the land, Husky coaches needed to get that point across to their own players. Long-time Holy Cross and later Seton Hall head coach George Blaney was in his third year as a Connecticut assistant. "Lots of them really did not believe how good they were," said Blaney.

Moore looked back at the six regular season losses for a team not expected to lose more than a few. "Only two losses really bothered me, the home loss to Providence and the loss at Notre Dame. Aside from those, we lost two games when Emeka had the back spasms and two others to very good teams at North Carolina and at Pitt."

Much of the pressure to win was on the shoulders of four-year starting point guard Taliek Brown. While he entered his senior season with seventy victories in his first three years and was the nation's winningest point guard, Taliek often was the focal point of fan disappointment. Before his final home game in Storrs, Brown said, "With me gone, who are they gonna talk about in chat rooms?"

Blaney recalled a story of how Calhoun could get a point across to a player while seemingly addressing someone else. "Jim was known for many things," said Blaney, "including

Freshman Charlie Villanueva shoots in the 2004 Final Four win over Duke. *(University of Connecticut Division of Athletics)*

coming up with new prayers. We are playing badly against Providence and in a moment when the crowd is silent, Jim shouts at referee John Cahill and says, 'Jesus, Mary, and Taliek' in order to get his message to his point guard."

An easy, but lackluster mid-February win over Miami in Hartford was punctuated by Calhoun's constant histrionics, which included kicking a sign near the team bench. He even waved to the crowd for support. "I felt like a jerk, by the way," said Calhoun. "It seems like I was the only guy going for awhile." Players and coaches alike signaled that the message was received that night, lasting for the rest of the season.

It was shown in the next game, as the Huskies applied the defensive clamps in beating Notre Dame 61–50 at the Civic Center to avenge the road loss twelve days before. The Irish shot 19 percent in the first half. The game featured a monster blocked shot by Okafor. He would make two buzzer-beating, game-saving blocks at Villanova a week later to preserve a 75–74 come-from-behind overtime win. It was UConn's first true comeback win of the season, trailing by 8 points with 7:15 left. More would follow in the five weeks ahead.

The final week of the regular season began with senior night. The work ethic of role players such as Tooles, Evanovich, and Ryan Swaller was warmly embraced by Coach Calhoun and a loud sell-out crowd. The next to last introduction was for soon-to-be graduate Emeka Okafor. Despite playing only three seasons, Okafor was an Academic All-American as a finance major. The final, well-deserved ovation was for Taliek Brown, as a four-year starter. Seton Hall, which later won an opening-round NCAA game, was a blowout victim by an 89–67 margin in front of a raucous Gampel Pavilion crowd.

But the bumps and bruises were not quite over. The regular-season finale was at Syracuse, where their seniors would be honored. The crowd of more than 32,000 was among the largest ever to see basketball in the Carrier Dome. The noise level cheering against the Huskies sounded like Gampel with three times the numbers. It was immediately evident that Okafor's back pain had returned. His play was ineffective, and he sat out most of the second half in a 67–56 Syracuse win.

It was the sixth loss of the season. With their star center again hurt, things looked bleak as the Huskies walked off the Carrier Dome floor. But perhaps an invisible genie tapped Calhoun on the shoulder and whispered, "That's it, Coach; that was your last loss of the year."

But it is not genies that bring championships—it is hard work. It is also stars and the supporting cast rising to the occasion. Calhoun started that theme on the trip home after the Syracuse loss. Preseason All-American Gordon had had an up and down year, partly due to a midseason broken nose and partly due to his unselfish, quiet nature, rather than aggressively taking over games. Tooles remembers the moment, "Coach Calhoun made it clear in front of all of us that it was time for Ben to step up—and for others to take up the slack starting at the Big East Tournament."

Others did indeed step up, none more than sophomore guard Rashad Anderson. A midseason injury to fellow sophomore Denham Brown opened the door for more playing time for Anderson. Evanovich described Anderson as a fun-loving guy, never bothered by pressure. Moore pointed out that the Huskies were 13–0 in Rashad's starts over the final fourteen games—the only loss, at Syracuse, was when he did not start. His self-confidence was obvious. "I always have confidence in myself," Anderson said. "A player of my caliber feels like every shot is going in. Once I get in rhythm, it's lights out." Husky fans saw that numerous times in the 2004 postseason.

But it was Gordon who immediately stepped up. With Okafor in street clothes for the opening Big East Tournament game against Notre Dame, Ben simply took over the game. It was a crucial game for the Fighting Irish as an NCAA Tournament "bubble" team, but Gordon poured in 29 points and freshmen Boone and Villanueva combined for 24 points and 29 rebounds in a 66–58 win that ended Notre Dame's NCAA hopes.

Okafor also sat out the next night when Gordon again scored 29 in an unexpectedly easy 84–67 semifinal win over Villanova. Anderson showed signs of what was to come by scoring 19.

Tooles thought the two Big East Tournament wins without Okafor were huge, setting up all that followed. But now the stakes were higher as their conference nemesis, regular-season champion Pittsburgh, awaited UConn in the title game. It was the third straight year the teams would meet in the Big East Tournament Championship game. In 2002 the Huskies won a double-overtime classic 74–65 with Brown hitting the shot of his UConn career—a 40-footer—to seal the win, but Pitt won the 2003 title game rematch, pulling away at the end 74–56. "Pitt was our toughest foe, every single time," said Tooles. Brown said it best, "Our team pretty much hates them."

Blaney said Pitt always forced the Huskies into a possession by possession–type game. "They take away your fast break, and they try to out-tough you, but we banged better with them in this year's championship than we had in the past."

With Okafor's back improved from rest and Villanueva unavailable due to an injured ankle the night before, Calhoun started his All-America center. The Huskies bolted to a 13–2 lead, but the Panthers took over after that and led at the half 34–25. With 8:23 to go, Pitt was up 51–40, but the Huskies went on a game-ending 21–7 run, led by Gordon, who hit the game winner in the lane with 30.2 seconds remaining. "They probably thought they had the win," said Gordon. "You could see those guys smilin' on the bench, laughing, and we just knew in our minds we're gonna *will* this win." While Okafor was huge off the boards with 13 rebounds, he fouled out with 2:19 to go and UConn down by two. Anderson made two important three-pointers down the stretch, including one from Hilton Armstrong's kickout pass that put the Huskies on top with two minutes left. "I told coach next time I touch the ball, I'm gonna make sure I stick it," Anderson said.

It gave the Huskies their sixth Big East Tournament title and fifth in the past nine seasons. Tourney Most Outstanding Player Ben "Madison Square" Gordon set a record for total points in the Big East Tournament with 81 in three games. UConn had thoroughly dominated Pitt at the game's start and finish in order to overcome being soundly outplayed in between. It was a pattern that would repeat itself two weeks later.

With six losses, UConn knew it would not be a number one NCAA seed, though the Big East Championship virtually assured a number two seed. What mattered even more would be the matchups, meaning avoiding the handful of teams whose style of play or recent hot streaks could cause an exit in the regionals. Highly ranked teams such as Kentucky, Oklahoma State, and Mississippi State looked to be worrisome, while the Huskies would match up very well against teams such as St. Joseph's and Stanford, both assured to be top seeds.

The newly named Phoenix Regional was the last to be shown on the CBS selection telecast. With UConn assigned a number two seed there behind Stanford, the instant analysts formed a near consensus that the Huskies should make it to the Final Four and were a strong candidate to win it all. Their opening rounds were to be played in Buffalo, oddly the same city where exactly fifty years earlier Hugh Greer's Huskies played in UConn's second-ever NCAA Tournament.

Jim Calhoun has never lost an opening-round NCAA game at UConn, but as his assistant coaches repeatedly say, he worries much more when a clear favorite. Of course the Huskies were just that against Vermont. The underdog Catamounts scored the game's first seven points, but Connecticut quickly took control after that, with Okafor holding Vermont star forward Taylor Coppenrath to just 3 for 17 shooting from the floor in a 70–53 win. By now Anderson's shooting was blazing, as he hit 6 of 9 three-point attempts for 22 total points to lead the scoring. Anderson stated why the whole team had jelled. "Once everybody bought into their role, we were a tough team to beat."

The 10 Greatest UConn Wins

While there were some wonderful wins in the 1950s, '60s, and '70s, it would be hard to argue against all ten of the greatest Husky wins being postseason games under Jim Calhoun. The list below includes the NCAA, NIT, and Big East Tournament (BET), all since 1988.

1. 1999 Duke NCAA Championship—a no-brainer top pick
2. 1999 Gonzaga NCAA Regional Final—a pulsating win to get to the Final Four
3. 2004 Duke NCAA Semifinal—12 straight points in final three minutes
4. 1988 Ohio State NIT Championship—the win that put UConn on the map
5. 2004 Georgia Tech NCAA Championship—the second Husky National Title
6. 1990 Syracuse BET Championship—first-ever league crown, a magic moment
7. 1990 Clemson NCAA Sweet Sixteen—the Tate George Shot
8. 1996 Georgetown BET Championship—final 12 points in thrilling comeback
9. 2002 Pittsburgh BET Championship—double overtime classic duel
10. 1988 West Virginia NIT first round—an overtime win that started it all

The next NCAA matchup was an emotional coaching event. Virtually no one had been closer to Jim Calhoun in his long coaching career than Dave Leitao, who first played for and later coached with Calhoun at Northeastern and spent fourteen seasons as a UConn assistant before taking Depaul's head coaching job in 2002. Leitao soon restored the Blue Demons to prominence, with a regular season cochampionship in the rugged Conference USA. This resulted in a seventh seed in UConn's regional.

"That was not fun," said Leitao. "The way they were playing, they looked unbeatable, and when the pairings came out, there was too much focus on Jim and me, and it took away from the players." It also did not help that the Blue Demons were forced into double overtime to win their NCAA opener over tenth-seeded Dayton.

"Our coaching styles are so similar that we could not do anything special against UConn," said Leitao. "And once we fell behind by 16 or 18 or so, it turned into something like an exhibition game." The Huskies had blown the game open early, leading 35–12 at one point late in the first half, and coasted to a 72–55 win, behind Gordon's 18 points.

What followed next was eerily similar to the 1999 route to the Huskies first Final Four. The venue was the same—the America West Arena in Phoenix, the game days were Thursday and Saturday as in 1999, the regional final game would again be the first of the four over the weekend, and UConn was by far the highest seed present, this time joined by sixth seed Vanderbilt, with the other regional semifinal between eighth-seeded Alabama and an old friend from the Big East, fifth-seeded Syracuse, the defending National

Champion. UConn's police-escort motorcycles even had special license plates: 1999.

What was not similar was the nature of the two games UConn played. Unlike the 1999 white-knuckle duels with Iowa and Gonzaga, the 2004 Huskies just rolled over the opposition. First up was an overmatched Vanderbilt team, and once again it was no contest by the half, with the Huskies up 45–27 leading to an easy 73–53 victory. Gordon had 20 points and 9 rebounds.

NCAA Regional Finals had traditionally been the most nerve-racking encounters for Husky supporters since the 1990 overtime loss to Duke. That was followed by regional final losses in 1995 to UCLA and in 1998 to North Carolina. After the 1999 regional final win over Gonzaga, UConn lost another tough one to eventual National Champion Maryland in 2002.

When Alabama defeated Syracuse in a mild upset by 80–71, UConn fans who had long memories could see the Crimson Tide looking a lot like the 1996 Mississippi State team that played forty minutes of near-perfect basketball to upset a top-seeded UConn team. Alabama was quick and very athletic and had played the nation's toughest schedule.

Perhaps a pregame chat with Anderson might have calmed some Husky fan nerves. He described the UConn powerhouse as they were playing in the NCAA Tournament, "You got Mr. Anderson on one hand shooting 50 percent from the three-point line in the tournament. You got Ben [Gordon] shooting 50 percent. You've got Emeka down low. You got Boone. You got so many weapons. Anybody could get 20 points a night."

John Gwynn was named "Microwave" by UConn's 1989–90 team for his knack of providing instant offense. But after the Huskies 2004 NCAA title, Gwynn told Anderson, "I give my title to you. *You* are the new 'Microwave.'" Gwynn explained, "His scoring ability is a little better than mine. His range is better than mine."

The opening half of the regional final against Alabama was, flat-out, the best twenty minutes of basketball played by any UConn team in a big game. Jim Calhoun praised his 1995 team, which went to the regional final, saying they played the best fast-break NCAA Tournament ball he had coached, but then he paused and added, "Until the 2004 team, of course."

Ending the first half against Alabama on a 15–2 run, the Huskies had put the game away by intermission at 53–29. The final score was 87–71, but the whole second half was "garbage time" since the victor had been decided. Anderson again caught fire from long range, with 6 of 9 from three-point land, five of them in the first half. CBS cameras caught him blowing on his finger in a pointed pistol image after one long three-pointer. Gordon continued his postseason scoring binge with 36 total, tying Ray Allen for the most points ever scored by a Husky in an NCAA game. Seldom had a team earned its way to the Final Four with four straight wins as convincing as these were.

As Connecticut returned to the Alamodome for its second-ever Final Four, Shamon Tooles recalled who was already at the other end of the floor. His Husky team was confident and had been made a two-point favorite, but Tooles recalled saying to himself as he looked at the opponent warming up, "That's Duke." For nearly the past twenty years, the Blue Devils had built up a mystique as the glamour program in college basketball. Until an unexpected overtime upset by Maryland in the ACC Championship game, Duke was ranked number one once again. Their road to the Final Four was a bit tougher than UConn's, especially their 66–63 regional final over a gritty Xavier team, but, as expected, they were there again—as it seemed like Duke was a Final Four team almost every year.

Yet that Duke mystique seemed to vanish at the game's start when UConn raced to a 15–4 lead in the first six and a half minutes—the opposite of falling behind the Blue Devils at the start of the 1999 championship game.

However, that initial run was marred by two fouls called on Emeka Okafor in the opening four minutes of play—the first a questionable call, the second close to ridiculous. The UConn coaching staff had only two real worries about the team's success in the 2004 tournament: Emeka's health and early foul trouble. The former resurfaced with a freakish new injury known as a shoulder "stinger" that took place in the first half of the Alabama rout. While Okafor was physically fine a week later for Duke, the early fouls placed UConn's title hopes in serious jeopardy.

Okafor's best friend on the team, Evanovich, spoke about his teammate. "He is a once in a lifetime person to know and was so focused, including in class." The CBS camera close-ups of Okafor as he waited out the final sixteen minutes of the first half showed the emotionally pained expression of someone who had worked so hard to just get to the Final Four in his home state and now felt denied by the officiating.

Calhoun spoke about the three memorable NCAA games with Duke in 1990, 1999, and 2004. Of the first two, including the heartbreaking regional final overtime loss in 1990, he said they were indeed classics and exceptionally well-played games. But as for the 2004 game, Calhoun's one word was "survival," meaning the questionable officiating, which eventually affected Duke via attrition of its big men. Calhoun has a strict two-foul rule, where players sit the rest of the first half after getting a second personal foul. "That rule might be twenty to twenty-five years old with me," said Calhoun. But with fouls mounting, Duke coach Mike Krzyzewski rolled the dice and left big men Shelden Williams and Shavlik Randolph in the game, and both had three personals by halftime.

After UConn's quick start and without having to face Okafor, Duke dominated the last thirteen minutes of the first half and took a 41–34 lead into the locker room. "I blew off steam for two or three minutes," said Okafor. "I didn't want to be a cancer for the team." Tooles added: "Emeka leads by example, but he spoke his piece at the half, and everyone clapped for him." Okafor scored all his 18 points in eighteen minutes after intermission.

But even with UConn's leader on the court, it looked like Duke's game. Daniel Ewing's three-pointer with 4:38 to go extended the Blue Devil lead to 73–64, but less than 30 seconds later Rashad Anderson countered with a three. After Duke made two foul shots and Okafor missed the front-end of a one-and-one, Duke had the ball, leading by eight with the clock showing under three minutes remaining. And then it all changed, totally changed.

Billy Packer on CBS called a three-point miss by Luol Deng, "Not the shot Duke wanted." The Huskies sprinted up court; open on the right beyond the three-point arc was that man Anderson again. He fired a long jumper in the instant he was open with 2:40 to go. As was so common in the 2004 title run, Anderson's three-pointer resulted in a huge momentum shift and cut the Duke lead to 75–70.

Another Ewing miss was followed by two Gordon free throws, then a steal by Josh Boone and a turnaround jumper by Okafor cut the lead to one. Still another stop by the Husky defense gave Connecticut the ball. As Okafor missed from the left of the basket, there was a scramble and Duke seemingly regained possession. However, the Huskies main man was not to be denied as Emeka simply used his exceptional strength to seize the ball away from Deng and score on a put-back to give UConn a stunning 76–75 lead with 26 seconds to go.

The next whistle went against Duke with only 12 seconds to go. Anderson had stripped the ball from Duke's J. J. Redick and calmly sank two foul shots putting the Huskies up by three. Still another missed Duke shot was followed by Okafor being fouled; he needed to sink only one of two and when the second went in, the Huskies had sealed the win with 12 straight points inside the last three minutes. UConn's defense made six consecutive stops. Anderson said, "We started hedging more on picks, cause we kept getting beat over the top on picks." Okafor scored 5 points in the final 78 seconds. UConn's Denham Brown said, "He changed the game in the second half with his offense and defense." A meaningless Duke three-pointer at the buzzer made the final score 79–78, the same as the 1990 classic, but this time it was the Huskies with the winning 79.

As he did in the Big East Tournament, the freshman Boone filled Okafor's shoes admirably, with 9 points and 14

Emeka Okafor jockeys for position against Duke. (University of
Connecticut Division of Athletics)

rebounds against Duke. "It was just like the Big East Tournament where we saw that everybody had to step up," Boone said. "It's one of the great wins we've had at UConn," said Calhoun.

Even though a game still remained, the Huskies joyfully celebrated the amazing comeback. The defeat stunned Duke and meant for the second time since 1999 the Huskies had denied the Blue Devils a national title. However, this time one more game remained, as Georgia Tech had won an equally close contest in the opening game by defeating favored Oklahoma State on a last-second shot, 67–65.

If any of the Huskies hadn't clearly remembered the 16-point loss to the Yellow Jackets in late November, ESPN Classic refreshed their memories. "We were in our hotel the night of the game," said Evanovich. "It was after our shootaround and before our pregame meal. We see a replay of our loss to them on TV, and it really fired us up. Watching it again, we could not believe how badly we had played in that game."

The Final Four had just enjoyed a thrilling semifinal Saturday with two last-second wins. In their analysis of the upcoming championship game on their Monday WFAN talk show, Chris "Mad Dog" Russo asked his partner Mike Francesa what the likelihood was of a third thriller. "Virtually none," was Mike's reply, and he was proven correct.

The Husky team that met Georgia Tech for the championship looked just like the same team that had blown away four NCAA opponents to get to San Antonio. As in those games, UConn's hot shooting and stifling defense put the game away in the first half. Still another three-pointer from Anderson before the halftime buzzer resulted in a

*Ben Gordon drives the lane against Georgia Tech in the 2004 NCAA
Championship Game.* (University of Connecticut Division of Athletics)

41–26 margin for intermission. "We fed off Emeka and our inside dominance," said Anderson. When it ballooned to 60–35, it was once again time for Connecticut to let the air out of the ball and watch the clock wind down. Several late three-pointers by the Yellow Jackets made the final score of 82–73 appear more competitive than the game actually was. Boone added 9 points and 6 rebounds, saying, "They beat us on the boards last time (November), and we realized if we were going to win this game, we were going to have to box out well and keep not only the big men, but their guards off the glass."

"They tried to press us a little bit," said Gordon, "and we took advantage of our team speed and got some easy buckets." Okafor, without foul trouble, led the team with 24 points and 15 rebounds, while Gordon finished his nine-game postseason scoring rampage with 21 points and the ever-present Anderson added 18. Emeka was named the Most Outstanding Player of the Final Four.

While being in the Final Four and winning it all was, of course, a thrill for each player, perhaps no one enjoyed it more than sixty-four-year-old assistant coach George Blaney. "Yes, it is a different thrill than playing," he said, "but I had been to thirty-eight Final Fours prior to this but never in any participating role. It was awesome just to be on the floor."

Tooles said, "The feeling at the very end was a bit weird. No one could quite believe we had finally won, even though all our work since the prior June had been to achieve just that."

Evanovich was candid about the celebrations: "We were more excited with the win over Duke, given who they

Jim Calhoun hoists his second national championship trophy. At right is sharpshooter Rashad Anderson. *(University of Connecticut Division of Athletics)*

were and the game itself." Indeed, the six-game journey to the 2004 championship will be somewhat remembered for five romps but mainly for those last three minutes against Duke.

Like Rashamel Jones five years before, Rashad Anderson was the one with the ball in his hands as the buzzer sounded for the second Husky National Championship. "I gave it to Emeka. I told him he had to give me his shoes to put in a case. Right after the game, I got them. They're home in Florida in a trophy case."

It sounds like it was a fair trade between two of the key players who made November's expectations a reality in early April.

About the Authors

Wayne Norman has been a UConn basketball and football radio commentator since 1979. His broadcasts with play-by-play announcer Joe D'Ambrosio are currently on WTIC, Connecticut's largest radio station, as well as a network of other stations throughout the state. Wayne also has the longest continuously running morning radio show in the state at UConn Network affiliate WILI-AM (1400).

Robert Porter is a 1971 graduate of UConn and a lifelong Huskies fan. While in college, he did play-by-play broadcasts of UConn basketball games for radio station WHUS. He has done freelance sportswriting for newspapers in Connecticut, and he works as an international banking consultant.